The S

The St Gargoyle's Diet

Ron

CANTERBURY
PRESS

Norwich

© Ron 2005

First published in 2005 by the Canterbury Press
Norwich (a publishing imprint of Hymns
Ancient & Modern Limited, a registered charity)
St Mary's Works, St Mary's Plain,
Norwich, Norfolk, NR3 3BH

www.scm-canterburypress.co.uk

All rights reserved. No part of this publication
may be reproduced, stored in a retrieval system,
or transmitted, in any form or by any means,
electronic, mechanical, photocopying or
otherwise, without the prior permission
of the publisher, Canterbury Press

British Library Cataloguing in Publication data

A catalogue record for this book is available

from the British Library

ISBN 1-85311-652-1

Typeset by Regent Typesetting, London
Printed and bound by
Bookmarque, Croydon, Surrey

Contents

For Elsie

Introduction

Once upon a time, more than a thousand years ago, there were two little villages. A Saxon called Shiva had built his *inga*, or homestead, where there was a spring, and others had joined him. Nearby, another Saxon called Affa, Uffa, or even Offa, had enclosed a bit of land, which became known as Affa's *penna*, or pen. Stay awake at the back. Over the years, Shiva Inga and Affa Penna became one village, and the name became corrupted, like all of us, and finally settled down to be Cheeving Halfpenny, so it really has nothing to do with money, or cheeving, or anything. But people come to see it because it sounds nice. It *is* nice. It has a pub, and a post office in the General Stores, and a butcher who sells sausages made from meat you'd actually eat even if he hadn't made it into sausages. And it has a primary school, and a church, the famous St Gargoyle's, named after a saint so obscure we don't even know when his day is, except that it's always a Friday. But it has a tower sixty-six feet high, and does its best to dominate the village.

Nearby, a couple of fields away, lies the little community of Ferret's Bottom, which was once just called The Settlement, because some gypsies happened to be there when the wheels fell off their wagons, so they stayed. Ferret's Bottom is still looked on with suspicion by the villagers of Cheeving, and the people at Ferret's Bottom encourage this, because it keeps Outsiders at bay, although the milkman, the postman, the doctor and the man who delivers propane gas all have fairly free access. Ferret's Bottom is part of the parish, and along with the village of Pighill (where the small church is dedicated to St Ickinsect), the other side of the Blicester–Huffleigh road, they form a benefice, and I'm the Vicar. Eight years behind the collar, man and boy.

Local delicacies, apart from the famous sausages, include Apple Cake, which is a cake with apples in it, or sometimes apples stuck together with cake, depending on whose recipe you follow, and a cheese called Blue Vinny, named after a footballer who swears considerably. The local people have never subscribed to the modern idea that food is bad for you, so portions tend to be huge, and the bus to Blicester for the Tuesday market is a heavy-duty vehicle with six wheels.

All this, that you're about to read (unless the lady in the shop asks 'Can I help you?' in that pointed way so you put it back on the shelf), happened the year the Olympic Games were held in Papaeete, which you heard little about, because there simply wasn't room for newspaper and sports reporters.

Chapter 1

Peas, perfect peas

Nothing much happens in Cheeving Halfpenny, mainly because it's in the middle of rural nowhere, and only has twelve hundred people, so there isn't really a lot of scope for things happening. The other parish in the benefice, Pighill, is even smaller, and nothing has ever happened there in all recorded history. And that's the way people seem to like it. If there were a burglary in Cheeving, it would probably be me that did it, because it's one of those villages where the Vicar is expected to do everything. We did have a Great Fire once, and a third of the village burned down, so we might have been famous for five minutes, but it was a Victorian fire, and it was upstaged in the news of its day by the Queen's Jubilee, or Jack the Ripper, or the Earl of Salisbury reshuffling his cabinet. The entire male population came home from a hard day skiving in the fields to find home burned to a shell. They gritted their teeth, built sheds, and got on with life. All the clothes they weren't actually wearing had gone up in flames, so things soon got a bit whiffy, it was said, all the water having been thrown on the fire by the women trying to put it out. If the people of Cheeving are tough, it's because they've

spent the last century or so hitting people who call
them smelly. There is only so much entertainment
to be had from a fire, even a Great Fire, so we have
learned to make our own amusements – quaint
rural pastimes like Watching TV, or Going Down
The Pub.

When the cottage opposite the Temporary Sign
(the village pub) was being re-thatched, we all did
Going Down The Pub, so we could sit outside and
watch. There we were, one hot Monday lunchtime,
under screaming swifts and whirling swallows, with
our pints of Busticles (the local ale), watching Something Happen. A man at work. Work is short in
Cheeving, which is a sore point with a lot of people,
and especially for those who can't find any to do, so
finding some to watch is the next best thing. Seeing
the thatcher up his ladder, like a tiny hairdresser
on a giant's head, ramming the straw into place,
pinning it down with those enormous hairgrips of
twisted hazel, and trimming it with huge shears,
was certainly good entertainment while it lasted.
Even when he hadn't slipped for several minutes,
he still held our interest. There isn't a lot of thatch
in the middle of the village now, on account of that
fire, so it has novelty value anyway, but all the old
men, especially, had some comment to make, com-
paring the current workman unfavourably with
craftsmen they thought they remembered. Or they
shouted that he'd put that last bit on upside down,
which is the local equivalent of wit. I half expected
them to hold up score cards like skating judges.
Even Mrs General, who had just shut the Stores for

lunch, paused a moment to admire the thatcher's broad shoulders, manly chest and cleavage, unable to keep a look of longing off her face.

Then along came Jason Orrell with Lennox the Rottweiler. Jason has a face like a badly stirred pudding of stubble and scars, with a sprinkling of studs and piercings, and a dog like a Tasmanian Devil, without any of that animal's more endearing qualities. He nodded to us all, tied Lennox's lead around one of those big green and white umbrellas, and went in to get a drink. He had walked across the fields from Ferret's Bottom, and obviously felt he'd earned it. Ferret's Bottom is a sort of suburb of Cheeving, and it was settled by gypsies some time before I moved here, and either has a quaint rustic charm, or is a haunt of lawless lowlife, depending on whether you're buying or selling. Jason had walked across the fields because coming around by the road would have meant passing the garage where he was supposed to be working for Derek Morris, but clearly wasn't.

I was only a little surprised to see him come out with a glass of red wine. For a man who was probably given lager in his baby mug, drinking red wine could mean only one thing. Jason had found the Lord. It had happened some months before, and now Jason wanted to be as much like him as possible. So although he said he was quite prepared to break a lifetime's habit and get a job, carpentry was the only thing he would consider at first, until Derek Morris, on my recommendation I have to say, reluctantly gave him a job as a mechanic. Jason has a way with cars, although since he became a Christian he hasn't had away with anybody else's. But trying to be like Jesus extended to drinks, too. If wine was good enough for Jesus, it was good enough for Jason. He joined us at our table, watched a big green and white umbrella chase Winnie's cat down the High Street, and then asked,

'So what car did he drive, Vicar?'

'Who?' I asked.

'The Lord Jesus,' he said, as if it was obvious. 'What car did he drive?'

Jason had read most of the Gospels, and considered there were serious gaps. Mark, he reckoned, had been especially slack. I was glad he'd brought the subject up, because there's nothing I like better than having a quiet pint on my day off interrupted by a theological discussion. The question I'm asked most often, apart from 'Do you want fries with that?' is probably about the source of evil in the world, followed by (in no particular order), how did God measure the first three days before he made the sun, do Buddhists go to heaven, what about the crusades, then, Vicar, and why did God make slugs. So 'What car did Jesus drive?' at least had the virtue of being original.

'He didn't drive,' I said. 'It was two thousand years ago. Even Mike's Fiesta wasn't around then.'

Mike Curly's Fiesta is a local legend. He never ever cleans it. It still has the general outlines of a Fiesta, but now it is so encrusted with good local mud that even the *Clean me* graffiti have silted up, and it sits there, lowering the tone of Ferret's Bottom, which

is difficult because in Ferret's Bottom a cat's tail is an optional extra. It is near impossible to get in or out of Mike's car without getting mud on the trousers from the sills, but Mike manages with the same sort of manoeuvring that Catherine Zeta-Jones does arriving at charity galas. Occasionally he rubs the worst off the number plates, so that the roadside speed cameras can note him passing through built-up areas at twenty-eight miles an hour, and so that we can all chuckle ironically at the registration, which reads C RAP. Mike was brought up the other side of London, in Dagenham, where rumour has it the car is actually worshipped on Saturdays, and he chose to express his atheism by pointedly watching sport on television while the rest of the population polished up its little tin gods, as he put it. As long as his car gets him to work and back, he is happy. It is neither status symbol, nor phallic symbol. It is simply his car, although legally it's agricultural land, and he claims a subsidy for it from the European Union as set-aside.

'If he didn't walk,' I said to Jason, 'Jesus rode a donkey.'

'Not even a horse, then?'

'No,' I said. 'He rode a donkey, to show he was humble, and not lording it over people. You can't feel lorded over by a man on a donkey, can you?'

Jason took a sip of his wine and pulled a face.

'Not a proper drink, is it?' he said. 'You sure he didn't drink lager?'

I assured him that there were no theological reasons for this, only that lager hadn't been invented then, and if he wanted to go back to drinking lager I wouldn't count it as a sin. Jesus, I said, would have drunk lager to show he wasn't la-di-dah like some people who drank wine. Jason knocked back his wine in one go, on the principle of waste not, want not, and disappeared for a minute. When he came back, he had a pint of lager in each hand, and a noticeable air of relief. I was just about to thank him for this unexpected bounty, when he called across the road to the thatcher on the roof.

'There's a beer for you here, mate!'

The thatcher was so startled he nearly fell off properly, but he recovered himself, came down the ladder so fast we heard his ears pop, and with a heartfelt 'Cheers!' in Jason's direction, downed more than half his pint most impressively.

Jason raised his own glass, saluting a fellow artist, then his features contorted into an expression I had come to recognize as thoughtful.

'So he'd have driven Mike's Fiesta, then,' he decided, half the glass later. 'If he'd been born a few years later. You can't feel lorded over by a bloke in a motorized dung heap, can you?'

Jason had started coming to church so that his marriage to Melony, which was getting nearer all the time, wouldn't be too much of a shock. Then he found, to his amazement, that he liked it, and then he decided to become a Christian. Some of the regular congregation were a bit put out, especially because he still smoked and drank heavily, but as he pointed out, there were no signs up in church saying he couldn't, and if anyone wanted to have fellowship with him in his six-pack they were more than welcome. I had at least managed to persuade him to wear a shirt in church, even on hot days, because he is heavily and elaborately tattooed. The Misses Tredgett, sitting behind him, said it was like being Greek Orthodox – if you couldn't understand the service, you could at least look at the pictures.

My glass was now empty, and despite my waving it about, nobody took the hint and said, 'Let me get you another one, Vicar,' so I said my goodbyes and left them to it. The old men gave me a surly nod, which is the equivalent, in these parts, of waving a handkerchief tearfully until you're out of sight, and prepared to enjoy themselves the way you can't when the Vicar is there listening.

As I passed Vineyard Cottage, one of the squatters who live there was fiddling with his motorbike, and as he saw me, whistled 'What a friend we have in Jesus', probably because he knew it's one of my favourites.

Hilary greeted me with her hands covered with flour.

'Did you get it?' she asked.

I must have looked blank. 'Sugar?' she prompted.

I confessed that Mrs General had just closed for lunch as I got there, because it had taken me longer than usual to get down the High Street because I had to walk the long way around the piles of dog mess, and all the motorbikes outside Vineyard Cottage, and then I'd seen the old guys outside the Temporary Sign and done my pastoral duty talking to them, and I couldn't not have a drink with them, could I? And then Jason came along and asked about Jesus, and so I'd actually been working on my day off.

Hilary sniffed, and said, 'I hope you like your apple pie on the tart side, then, because I was counting on that sugar.' I said tart would be fine by me.

'What are your plans for this afternoon?' she asked, and before I could invent anything, Hilary said we could go shopping, and still be back in time to collect the boys from school.

'Not Blicester?' I said. 'I can't face Blicester on a hot afternoon.'

'No,' said Hilary. 'Food shopping. We can go to Saneways in Huffleigh.'

Huffleigh is only about fifteen miles away, and food shopping I don't mind, because it's air-conditioned, and I get to choose the breakfast cereal, and if I make enough fuss at the checkout, Hilary might buy me an Aero to keep me quiet.

So as soon as the pie was out of the oven, and before it was cool enough for me to be tempted to set upon it, we set off, narrowly missing a man at the bottom of the Vicarage drive who was nailing

a fluorescent yellow notice to
the telegraph pole. I resolved
to look at it on the way back,
and take down the one for
the coffee morning, which
had been a month ago. The
telegraph poles in the village
are all studded with pins and
staples because everybody
advertises everything on them. Very few people
think to take them down afterwards, and I'm afraid
St Gargoyle's is no better than anybody else in this
respect.

Two hours later we were £70 poorer, and Hilary
had refused to buy me an Aero because it was too
soon after lunch, too soon before supper and anyway I could do with losing a bit of weight, not
putting any more on. I was thinking how much
I hate supermarkets. The girl at the checkout,
who needed a label to remember her name was
Tina, knew the price of everything just by whiz-
zing it through her little scanner. Except for one
item, which she held up and shouted, 'Nit combs!
How much are nit combs?' at the top of her voice.
Hadn't she ever heard of the seal of the confession-
al? She was wearing a yellow smock with the face
of Sammy Saneway on it, and the slogan 'You'd be
Mad to Pay More!' Sammy Saneway is cross-eyed
and his tongue hangs out, so he looks as if he's just
been hung.

'Is that true?' I asked Tina, pointing in the region
of her bust.

'It's what the manager told me when I asked for a rise,' she said morosely. '"I'd be mad to pay more," he said.'

I was reading the yellow notice at the bottom of the drive. It was from the District Council, inviting me to their offices in Huffleigh, where we'd just come back from, to examine the plans of an application by Saneway Supermarkets, where we'd just been spending the stipend.

The really bad news was, the planning application was in respect of the field adjoining the churchyard, and, come to that, the Vicarage back garden. The prospect of having a supermarket just the other side of the larch-lap wasn't an attractive one. There was only one thing for it, I decided. First thing in the morning I would call on Ted Gruntle, the farmer who owned the field.

It was a trying evening, washing the boys' hair with that special shampoo, and then trying to stop them playing with matches. We warned them that the alternative was shaving them bald, so they looked like the cast of Oliver! They subsided into sullen submission.

'The trouble is,' Hilary said that night when we were getting ready for bed, 'you don't have any will-power.' She was eyeing my abdomen as if it might do something worse than just stretch my shirt a bit.

'True,' I said. 'I try, but it doesn't seem to work.'

'Back in Lent,' she said, and I knew what she was going to remind me of, 'you did that sponsored slim, and by Easter, you'd actually put on four pounds.'

I smiled complacently. 'But most people gave me the sponsor money anyway,' I said. 'Because they'd already made up their mind they were going to.'

'You didn't deserve it,' she said.

'Exactly. And I got a sermon out of it too,' I said. 'The actual amount of our sin doesn't come into it, and all our trying to be good doesn't work because we're weak and only human. And God forgives us anyway, not because we deserve it, but because he wants to, and because he feels sorry for us.'

Hilary gave the snort of a woman who recognizes dodgy theology when she hears it, and picked up her copy of *Practical Eavesdropping*. The steady thump of heavy metal music drifted up the drive and into our bedroom window, because Vineyard Cottage is just over the road at the bottom of the drive. The hedge filtered out a decibel or two, but it still sounded like fairy harpists throwing dustbins at each other.

'The squatters are noisy,' remarked Hilary. 'Are you sure there's only eight of them?'

'They've probably got friends in,' I said. 'They daren't all go out, because they won't leave the place empty. That's why they can't go to work, either, poor things.'

'How do you get four couples in a cottage that size?' Hilary wondered.

'Perhaps they share bedrooms,' I suggested.

Then I had a terrible thought. 'Would you still love me if I was fat?' I asked.

'If?' she said, doing that raising-one-eyebrow thing she does.

'But would you?'

'Don't put it to the test,' she said.

Chapter 2

Amazing grapes

First things first. Tuesday morning means Assembly at the village school, a high point in any vicar's week, as it gives him the opportunity to conduct an act of worship with teachers keeping order, so there is none of the unruly coughing, shuffling and whispering, paper dart throwing and fighting that the Sunday congregation in church usually indulges in.

So I found my rubber snake, to illustrate St Paul's adventure on the beach of Malta (striking terror into their little hearts never does any harm, in my experience), and set off.

All was quiet at Vineyard Cottage after the noise of the night before. There is usually little activity until mid-morning. Vineyard Cottage is owned by Major Stern, of the Earl of Wessex's Regiment, and when he went off to Belize a couple of years ago he let it to a young couple, who paid rent for a little while, then stopped. Three other couples moved in with them, and four large bikes, which had originally been Harley Davidsons, but were now so heavily modified their own mothers wouldn't recognize them. The eight squatters were variously shaved, tattooed and pierced, even the men. They made Jason look like an amateur. They wore denim and leather, and did no noticeable work. When it rained, the water ran in oily rainbows down the High Street. Their taste in music was heavy metal bands with names like Cholera, Steel Dog and AD/BC (I think). I turned away, and headed for the school.

Outside the school gate there was the usual tantrum.

'I don't want to go to school!' Tiny feet stamped.

'But you have to go.' Her mother was firm but kind.

'Waagh! I hate school!' Hands were now clenched into fists.

'Now now, don't take on.' Mother was trying now to console, rather than threaten.

'Why do I have to go to school?' Rage had now given way to sullen resentment.

'Because you're the head teacher.'

I went inside and left them to it.

There they all were, sitting cross-legged on the hall floor, wearing the uniform red sweatshirt, and all sporting jolly red and yellow badges with their names on. These were new. The badges had a face, with cross eyes and a waggling tongue, which looked vaguely familiar. Then it clicked – this was Sammy Saneway, the face of the supermarket chain that was planning to build on Ted Gruntle's field. It was seeing it out of context that threw me. Like when you bump into the Duchess of Gloucester in the off-licence, her face doesn't register straight

away. And here were Saneways, giving badges to the schoolchildren. Which struck me as a good idea, as very often I don't know who the children are, even though I baptized half of them. They looked different then, which is my excuse.

The children were suitably impressed by St Paul not swelling up and turning blue when the snake bit him, although there was some consternation when he shook it into the fire, which a lot of them thought was a waste of a good snake. Little girls played 'Jesus' hands were kind hands' and 'One more step along the world I go' on squeaky recorders. Hell is, I'm sure, full of little girls with squeaky recorders. We said prayers, and wished everybody a happy birthday, whether they'd had one or not. I said goodbye to them and left. Miss Jolly heaved a great sigh of relief that everything had gone without

a hitch. Miss Jolly's idea of a good assembly is one
that doesn't have half the children asking questions
afterwards that won't be on the syllabus for another five years.

A quick cup of coffee back home while I looked
through my mail, all of which I threw away except
a cheque from the monumental mason for a small
vase not exceeding 305mm x 203mm, and then I was
off to see Ted Gruntle. There have been Gruntles in
Cheeving Halfpenny for four thousand years. Ted
insists that the long barrow on his farm was built
for, and by, Stone Age Gruntles, and that the skel-
eton in the museum in Blicester that came from the
round barrow by the main road was a Bronze Age
Gruntle. ('Look at his teeth,' Ted says, as if that
clinched the matter.) The Romans built the Iron
Age Gruntles a nice house so they didn't have to
live in a mud hut any more, and when the Romans
left to deal with troubles nearer home, the Gruntles
slipped back into their old ways, except for con-
verting to Christianity somewhere about this time.
Wars and civil wars hardly disturbed them, and
their way of life continued almost unchanged until
the last-but-two of the Gruntles had electricity laid
on just in time to hear Mr Chamberlain say there
was a proper war, one he could join in. Being a
farmer, he turned the invitation down, and Dug for
Victory instead. The history of the Gruntles is the
history of Cheeving Halfpenny, and now Ted, the
last Gruntle but one, owns the farm that extends
right up behind the village to the north. Although
the farmhouse is just out of the village, the field

behind the churchyard belongs to him. Or did. I
followed the sound of bleating, and found him in
the barn, drooling the sheep. The noise was deaf-
ening, and the smell of the hot drooling-iron filled
the echoing space. We don't see Ted in the village
very much, because the farm takes up a great deal
of his time and energy. When he does appear in
the Temporary Sign he's friendly enough, although
some people keep their distance. Bear in mind that
he still tells anyone who will listen that he once had
a talking carrot, that would sit on his shoulder and
say 'Critty Colly'.

As soon as I could after the requisite small-talk,
comments on the weather, and the prospects for
harvest, I brought up the subject of the field.

'It wasn't so much that I sold it, Vicar,' he said,
struggling with an undrooled ewe, 'as they just
come along and bought it. I never put it on the
market, they just came along and asked. And what
with the price of everything being so low, what
they offered me would keep me in a manner I'd like
to become accustomed to long enough for me to
become accustomed to it. So I said yes.' The drooling complete, he let the ewe go, and she staggered
off with as much dignity as she could muster under
the circumstances.

'Did you know what they were planning to do
with it?' I asked him. He seized the next ewe, and
tested the drooling-tongs on his welly. They melted
a small hole in it, which appeared to be satisfac-
tory.

'I didn't even know who they was,' he said, with

Sheep worrying

a shrug of his enormous shoulders that nearly split the back of his jacket. 'That field is so far away from here I need me passport to get up there to plough it. I thought set-aside were a good idea, but selling it was even better.'

'A supermarket will be almost as big as the village,' I said. 'I've not seen the plans yet, but if it's anything like the one in Huffleigh, it will be like the North Terminal at Gatwick.'

'Ain't seen that,' said Ted. 'Flew from Heathrow, I did. Besides, it isn't my problem any more. I won't miss that field, and it's made me more than I could have earned in the rest of my life, farming.'

'So you won't be drooling any more sheep,' I said, wincing.

'Oh yes, I will,' he said. 'That's different. A spot of drooling's better than *Inspector Morse*. Besides, there's young Paul.'

Paul is his son, who works the farm now, because one day it will be his. I couldn't stand to watch any longer, so I left Ted to his grisly work, and walked back to the village. As the memory of the drooling wore off, I found my appetite returning, and popped into the General Stores for a packet of Hula Hoops. Mrs General was in animated conversation over the counter with Mrs Macreedy, and they both looked up as the door bell tinkled.

'Ah, Vicar,' said Mrs General. 'Have you heard about the Plans?'

I said I had, but didn't know the details. Mrs General was so indignant, not only were her arms akimbo, but everything else was akimbo, too.

'We can't be having a supermarket here,' she said. 'This is my livelihood, Vicar,' she said. 'Who's going to pay my outrageous prices when they can get things much cheaper in Saneways?'

'Maybe that's not the best way to put it,' I suggested. 'Maybe what you should be saying is that the village Stores is part of the very fabric of the rural community, with its emphasis on personal service and fresh, locally grown produce.'

Mrs Macreedy snorted. 'I only came in to complain these bananas were past it,' she said, 'but I do see your point. We don't want a supermarket in Cheeving.'

'That's right, Vicar,' said Mrs General. 'You've got away with –'

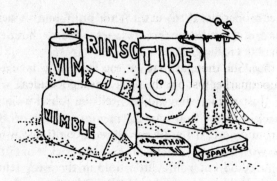

'Not true,' I interrupted. 'That was just a rumour put about by the Methodists.'

'– words,' she said. 'You've got a way with words. If we get up a campaign to stop Saneways desecrating the village, will you be our chairman?'

I said I'd have to think about that one, or at least see the plans first. I have enough on my plate, like Sunday's sermon, the summer fête, and the readers' rota, without getting involved in yet another unequal battle between simple rural folk who just want to be left in peace and a faceless retail giant backed by greedy corporate lawyers, to prevent the despoliation of a charming and idyllic corner of England. But I bought my potato-based snack, and a bag of sugar, and promised them I'd go and look at the plans, and see if there were real grounds for an objection.

Hilary had just finished mucking out the boys' room. The easiest way to do this would be to divert a small river through it for a day or two, but there isn't one handy, so it's all down to hard manual labour. She pushed back her mask and peeled off her rubber gloves to put the kettle on. While we were having a cup of coffee, she suggested we both go over to Huffleigh and look at the plans in the council office. She thought that, on the face of it, having a supermarket just out the back was a good idea.

'Just think,' she said, 'there'll be jobs for local people. Everybody says there aren't enough jobs around here. If I got a job there, I could just walk to work.'

'I could cut you a little hole in the back fence and you'd be there,' I said. 'But Mrs General just asked me to chair a committee to oppose the whole idea.'

Her face clouded. 'And you said no, because the Vicar has to be completely impartial?'

'Not if it's a moral question,' I said. 'Then it's the Vicar's duty to do the right thing. Support the good against the evil.'

'Supermarkets aren't evil,' she said. 'So why is it more evil for a supermarket to be here rather than anywhere else?'

'I didn't say they're evil,' I said. 'But I'm sure there's a moral side to the question.'

'So do you ask yourself, does God want a super-market in Cheeving?'

'I don't know whether God wants supermarkets at all,' I answered. 'God might prefer it if people in Sri Lanka grew stuff they could eat, rather than tea for us to drink. Or that we didn't waste energy driving over to Huffleigh to buy stuff, and big trucks didn't waste even more taking it there in the first place.'

'Will you ask him about it tonight when you say your prayers?'

'I'll certainly think about it,' I said.

'Why I like being married to you,' said Hilary, standing up and ruffling my hair, 'is that we don't have time to discuss what's happening in *EastEnders*.'

'I bought you some sugar,' I said.

'That was sweet of you,' she said, 'but we picked some up yesterday when we were in Saneways. And you've already eaten the pie, if you remember.'

I remembered. It was a very good pie. A little on the tart side, maybe, but most acceptable. Hilary asked if I was going to look at the plans that afternoon. But when I looked in my diary, I saw I was due to speak to the Mothers' Union the next day about the Manichaean Heresy, so I ought to at least look it up and see what it was. The trouble is, when you read about heresies, they seem quite reasonable, and you realize there are people in the clergy chapter who think the same way. So seeing the plans would have to wait. Still, it's always nice to have something to look forward to.

Chapter 3

What a friend
we have in cheeses

Nothing much happens in Cheeving Halfpenny. Not even the Women's Institute. We have a Mothers' Union branch which flourishes around the church, and at least half the members are in the WI as well, but the Women's Institute meets in Huffleigh. Alice is a member, and so is Jean, and Jean is usually quite happy to drive. But when she broke her arm in a bizarre gardening accident – well, it wasn't really bizarre. She was carrying one of those big bags of John Innes, hugging it to her chest, so she never saw the fork, and tripped over it. The bag of compost broke the fall of everything except her arm, which the fall broke. Anyway, driving was out of the question, and Alice particularly wanted to go to the talk on caring for tropical lizards. Her husband Robbie, an expatriate Scot who came here as a shepherd and never went back because Alice, for some reason, thought Scotland was full of wild hairy men who got drunk on a regular basis, agreed to drive her over to Huffleigh, and he would have a wee drink in the Knife and Rabbi across the road from the Memorial Hall. She could come and fetch

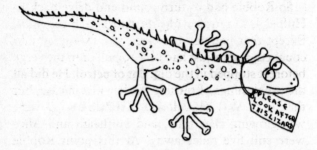

him when she had absorbed all there was to know about tropical lizards and the care thereof.

Alice appeared in due course, full of reptilian lore. Robbie drained his pint, stubbed out his cigarette, and they got into the car, which refused to start. He tried the ignition again, and it still refused. This was not surprising, as in the bright early evening in the car park when they arrived, Robbie had failed to notice he had left his lights on. He asked Alice to get out and push, which she did, reluctantly, with her backside to the boot, until she was practically running down the road backwards. The car grunted into life.

I was on my way to Huffleigh, a man with a mission, and I was hardly past Gruntles' Farm when I saw Robbie with a petrol can. I gave him a lift, and he told me the story, and what happened next, and why he expected to be in the doghouse for a whole week.

'When we got home,' he said, 'I said to her, "Are ye no goin' tae get out and open the gate?" She didnae answer, and when I looked, she wisnae there!'

So Robbie had to turn round and drive back to Huffleigh to retrieve Alice from the pub car park. Except that halfway there, the car spluttered and coughed, and he just had time to pull onto the verge before it stopped in the dip, out of petrol. He did all the usual things of turning the key just in case, but the needle was hard down, the little orange light was glowing cheerfully, and Huffleigh and Alice were still five miles away. At this point Robbie gave way to despair, and did all the usual things – banging his head on the steering wheel, cursing his folly and improvidence, and offering God a deal, as we all do, as if we had anything to offer God that he doesn't already have, or we ought to be giving him anyway. It was while he was banging his head that he became aware of another banging. This time it was on the car window, and when he looked up, the face peering in was Alice.

Alice had gone back into the Rabbi, found Gerry Martin, who lives in the village, and begged a lift home from him. And spotting the car on the side of the road, they stopped and picked up Robbie, which Alice said was more than he deserved, but she didn't have her house key with her, and needed his. Alice is a saint, really. I discovered that when I found her once thanking God out loud for curing the cat's constipation at the same time that she was mopping the kitchen floor. But this morning, Robbie thought that he had used up his stock of goodwill, even from the saintly Alice, so he had made her a cup of tea, taken the can of petrol he kept in the garage for the mower, and would have walked the

ten miles to his car if I hadn't stopped and picked him up. I heard his confession, as it were, waited while he poured the petrol into the tank, and made sure he was on his way, then off I went. Even giving someone a lift made me feel like a good scout, because all too often I get the impression that vicars can't do a great deal, and what's worse, everybody else knows it.

The planning office isn't actually in Huffleigh. The Town Hall, in the market place, has a colonnaded entrance and it gets used for the Farmers' Market, blood donation and begging. The planners moved out a few years ago, fatter, paler and without any loose change, to new offices down a lane just the other side of town, to make it more difficult for people to come and see plans, in case they want to object. To make themselves even more secure, the little sign at the T-junction pointing to the District Council Offices actually points the wrong way, and is upside down into the bargain.

A man with a degree in surly and a uniform cap directed me to an office on the top floor. There, a map of the whole county covered one wall, and there was a desk with a bell you could hit if you felt the need to hit something, and still had the energy to. But there was a girl behind the desk already, eating a bag of Quavers, and I asked her if I could see the plans for the supermarket in Cheeving Half-penny. She asked me what the reference number was.

I said I hadn't a clue, and she said she couldn't find the plan without a reference number. I asked her very nicely if she could try. She gave a sigh that would have put out a candle at ten paces, and stomped off. Just as I was beginning to feel the need to hit something, and wondering if the bell would do, she came back with a folder the size of an atlas, and said I could look at it there but not take it away.

The church wasn't even on the drawings. There was a supermarket, sure enough, with a huge car park, service bays, loading bays and its own access road off the High Street, right next to the Vicar-age drive, but nothing at all to suggest there was a church just over the dotted line that represented the wall; or a Vicarage, or, indeed, a village. I'd pinched a piece of Hilary's greaseproof paper, and the girl didn't object to me tracing the site plan. The rest of the drawings showed elevations, sections, and all

the detail needed to show that this would be a fine asset to any industrial estate on a ring road, and a marked improvement to somewhere like Swindon, but not to a village like ours. I wrote down a couple of addresses, made a note of that important reference number, tried to keep the irony out of my voice as I thanked the girl for her help and co operation, and headed for home.

I stopped off on the way to exorcise the evil spirits from the cupboard under Mrs Treadwell's stairs. They put up quite a struggle, because her old hockey stick from school is under there, along with her late husband's Gunn and Moore three-springer. So by the time I reached the High Street I was feeling spiritually drained and hungry. I thought a Twix would deal with one, and a couple of chapters of Isaiah the other. I still had the Mothers' Union to address in the afternoon, and I wasn't convinced they would all stay awake, or even if I would. But halfway up the High Street, before I got to the Stores, I noticed there was a crowd on the wide bit just in front of the telephone exchange, so I went to see what was the big attraction. At first I thought another alien spacecraft had landed, but then I saw it had wheels.

Big Jim lives alone in the farmhouse down the lane opposite the school. He would be Something Big in the City, if he didn't do the whole thing at home with his computer and the Internet. Here he was, looking considerably smaller than usual, because he was in the driving seat of this huge pink, white and chrome confection, surrounded by an incredulous crowd. A crowd in our village, by the way, is nine people.

When I asked him, Jim explained, probably for the twenty-eighth time, that it was a 1959 Cadillac Eldorado Biarritz.

'Ah,' I said. 'A fifty-nine,' as if I were a connoisseur of classic American automobiles. I walked around it. It took a little while. You needed good boots and Kendal Mint Cake to walk around this car. The bows were a sort of club sandwich, with extravagant lights and a grille you could only clean with a toothbrush, and below that, the same again, only this time in chrome. Yards behind that, the stern rose into a pair of vast triangular fins, chest high, adorned with arrays of red lights shaped like nuclear warheads. In between, the bonnet and boot shone like the crystal sea in Revelation, and right in the middle, on a white leather sofa, sat Jim, looking pretty pleased with himself, because, as I found out later, this incredible car cost more than some of the cottages in the village.

'Business is good, then?' I asked.

Jim smiled. 'Business is all right,' he said.

And then I'm afraid I wiped the smile off his face by asking, 'What does it do to the gallon, then?'

'Why is everybody asking what it does to the gallon?' he cried, banging the steering wheel with both hands. 'You want an economy car, you drive your widdling little Fiat! I bought this because I love it. All my life I've wanted one of these, and now I have. What it does to the gallon has nothing to do with it at all!'

And then he added, in a sheepish little whisper, 'Eight.'

I guess the image of God is strong in Big Jim. God doesn't love us because we're useful, or economical, but just because he does. It's true, I drive a Fiat Amoeba, because it does lots of miles to the gallon, but I can't say I love it. It just does its job. But Jim is an enthusiast, like God, rubbing his hands with anticipation of being with us, and in us, taking us for a burst around the block.

There was Jason, still there as the crowd began to melt away so that Jim could at last drive off.

'That's it, isn't it, Vicar?' he said.

'What's that?' I asked.

'That's the car Jesus would have driven.'

The talk on the Manichaean Heresy went down very well, thank you for asking. Most of the ladies were totally absorbed, closing their eyes in deep concentration. At the end, when I asked if there were any questions, Mrs Tooley asked, 'If matter is actually evil, does that mean fat people are more evil than thin ones?'

I looked through my notes to see if I'd actually said anything that might have given that impression.

'If stuff is bad and only spirit is good,' said one of the Miss Tredgetts, who bribed their way into the Mothers' Union for the ginger nuts, 'then the more stuff you have,' and she looked across at Mrs Groves, who hasn't seen her knees since the Silver Jubilee, 'the more evil you must be.'

'It was a heresy,' I pointed out. 'It wasn't actually true. They were trying to say that Jesus couldn't have been really human because that would have meant him being physical.'

'Nothing wrong with being physical,' said Mrs Groves, with a look that defied anyone to argue. I made my excuses and slid out, vowing that next time I'd talk about something less controversial, like women bishops or homosexuality.

Beside the bench at the war memorial, there was a pair of boots, or what had been a pair of boots once, but was now approaching toxic waste. I resolved to come back and deal with them, the way I'd deal with a dead badger. I'm used to the odd beer can by the bench, but boots were a new departure.

Hilary greeted me, surrounded by the scent of air-freshener, and with the air of someone who has heard news, and has been frustrated by having nobody to tell it to.

'Shane Bloat has been arrested,' she said before all of me was through the front door. I asked what for, although there were all sorts of possibilities. Shane had upheld Ferret's Bottom's tradition of lawlessness with great enthusiasm. Poaching was merely a sideline. Shane couldn't do complicated things like credit-card fraud or hacking into building society computers, but there was always burglary, taking and driving away (which is the technical term for stealing cars), and taking things from cars if he didn't want the whole thing, or if all else failed, simply causing a breach of the peace. Yet somehow the police were never able to catch him at it, or with it, or whatever was needed to secure a conviction.

'Selling tax discs,' said Hilary, 'while not being Pete at the post office.' Apparently the post office at

Griping St Todger had been robbed a week before, and Shane had been caught trying to sell a tax disc to an off-duty policeman who couldn't believe his luck. A felon in the cells *and* a cheap tax disc! I made a note to go and see Shane's father, Darkie, and offer what sympathy I could muster. The boys rushed downstairs, also bursting with news.

'We had a tramp for tea,' they said.

'Did you save me any?' I asked.

'He was really, *really* smelly,' they said. 'And he had sausage, egg and chips and a sandwich to take away. And he was wearing really smart trainers.'

I looked surprised, but Hilary nodded confirmation. 'Really smart ones. Expensive, and new.'

'Which explains why there's a pair of ex-boots abandoned by the war memorial,' I said. 'I'll move them in the morning, if they haven't run off by themselves. They could cost us the Best Kept Village prize.'

Later that night, after I'd put the cat out, I gave the boys a solemn lecture. The cat did not have nits. The nit shampoo is highly inflammable. Inflammable doesn't mean you *can't* set fire to it, it means you *can*. Let this be a lesson to you. I might as well have saved my breath. I heard them giggling later about having a cat that goes 'Woof'.

Chapter 4

Crust and obey

Nothing much happens in Cheeving Halfpenny, so the day Mrs General let off all her debtors will be remembered long after the day we had the meeting about the supermarket has been forgotten, even though they were the same day. It was the next Monday. It's a good job I don't go away too often on my day off, or I'd miss half of what does happen. I only received my call-up the day before. When people make the usual joke about me only working one day a week, I always say, 'You don't mean Sunday, do you? I don't work Sunday – I worship God on Sunday, and that isn't work!' which sometimes shuts them up. Anyway, we were in the vestry after the morning service, feeling pretty good because it had gone really well. Nobody had tripped over anything, the choir had sung like angels and even the boys had been inconspicuous, which is the most I ever expect of them. I remember once when St Paul was sounding off to Timothy how a church leader should be a person who could control his family, the boys started an actual fist fight in the pew, and resisted all my efforts to break it up.

I signed the service register, and noticed that the Colonel had put the attendance down as fifty-eight and a half.

'How can you have a half?' I asked. 'Has some-one had a leg off and didn't tell me? Did someone leave while my back was turned?'

The Colonel was picking the buttons and foreign coins out of the collection, and muttering that there was no call for pesetas at all now, even in Spain, and definitely not in our collection. He looked up. 'Didn't you know? Mary Lucas is four months' pregnant.'

Adrian was still struggling to get out of his cassock without undoing it because he's a born-again lazy perisher, and I was trying to get my risible off over my head without disturbing what's left of my hair. Adrian asked me, 'When you put your stole on, why don't you kiss the little cross on it like Father Bruce does?'

'Because I don't have to,' I said. 'Jesus says I just have to look on it lustfully, and he takes it that I've kissed it.'

Before he could work out whether or not I was joking, and while I was trying to remember who Father Bruce is, Shirley put her head round the vestry door and said Mrs General wanted a word. As Mrs General never openly comes to church, only sneaks in to make her own private devotion I'll tell you about sometime, I was intrigued. She was waiting for me by the coffee area, looking disapprovingly at our coffee, because we only serve Fairtrade, which she doesn't sell.

But first I had to say goodbye to Myrtle. Every-body else gets a handshake as they leave the church. Myrtle has Down's syndrome, and she's thirty-six, or just nine, depending how you count, and insists on a kiss.

'See you next Sunday,' she said. She never stays for coffee, because she has to go and make a sandwich for Big Jim. Mrs General was at my elbow.

'Hello, Vicar,' she said. 'Sorry to disturb you on your busy day, but we're having a meeting, and we need you to be there.'

'Now?' I said. 'It's nearly lunchtime.'

'Not today,' she said. 'One evening.'

'Jolly good,' I said. 'There's nothing I like better than meetings in the evening, and I've only got five this week. What's it about?'

'The supermarket,' she said. 'We've got copies of the plans, and we need to organize our protests and objections. You said you'd be our spokesman.'

'I did?'

'Yes, on Tuesday.'

I remembered. Sometimes you don't have to step forward to volunteer, only stand still while everyone else steps back.

'So we'll see you tomorrow evening at the New Hall.' She turned to go.

'Hang on,' I started to protest. 'Monday's my day off.'

'But this isn't to do with you being the Vicar,' she said. 'This is just about you being a member of the community. See you tomorrow.'

And off I went to take the eleven o'clock service at St Ickinsect's at Pighill. I have no idea how I came to be given another parish. When an archdeacon says he's concerned about your career

development, watch out. It means he doesn't think you're working hard enough, and hands you another parish like the dealer at pontoon. Anyway, I would very likely have forgotten all about Mrs General and the meeting, except I saw her on the Monday, because I called in at the Stores for a loaf. There was obviously something exciting going on, because there were about a dozen people in the shop and around the open door. It doesn't take many people to look like a crowd in our village, and as I said, nine is the official number, so I think, technically, this was a throng.

Mrs General was explaining something with great patience to people who were finding the concept difficult to grasp.

'No, I'm not making a new one,' she was saying. 'I'm just doing away with this old one.'

'So how will you know who owes what?' asked Mrs Pershore.

'I won't,' said Mrs General. 'As from today, nobody owes me anything.'

'But I owe you a bit,' said Mrs Tremblett uncertainly.

'A fair bit,' agreed Mrs General. 'Can I have it?'

'Well, no,' Mrs Tremblett said, 'because I haven't got it.'

'There you go, then,' said Mrs General. 'That's why I'm stopping the whole thing. No more day book, nobody owes me anything, everybody's let off. Spread it around. As from now, cash only, no tick, and this' – she held up the tattered exercise book that detailed the debts of half the village – 'goes in the bin.' Which it did, with a thud.

There was a gasp from the half-dozen people in the shop, which spread to those outside. In the confusion I managed to buy a small wholemeal that looked like an elephant's dropping, paid cash with a flourish, and asked Mrs General what that had all been about.

'The day book. The tick. I got so fed up with asking people to pay off what they owe, and they never do. Some people have stopped coming in at all because they're embarrassed. Not that Mrs Pershore, mind you. If she'd paid me all she owed me, I could have retired by now. And you never know but I might need all the customers I can get, so I've just written off the whole thing. They all think it's a stunt, but I was just sick of it. It can't cost me anything, 'cause I was never going to get the money anyway. See you tonight,' she said pointedly, 'at the meeting!'

Outside the shop, people were still talking about Mrs General's amnesty. The consensus of opinion, voiced by Mrs Pershore, was that it was some sort of trick, and nobody just lets everybody off just like that. I didn't wait to discuss the theological implications of that, because now I had the raw material, I was anxious to make a sandwich.

And in the evening, I tore myself away from *Celebrity Surgery* to go round to the Hall. I asked Hilary to keep an eye on it, so she could tell me if the patient recovered from having a triple heart bypass performed by a woman who used to be in *Hi-de-Hi*. I would have taken the car, but Hilary was still making remarks about the tightness of my waistband, and suggested I walk. As it happened, they needn't have bothered hiring the New Hall, which had risen eventually, if a little unsteadily, out of the ashes of the old one, but curiously always smells a little smoky. There were only six of us there, and we could have met in the Temporary Sign, and then Arthur could have been there and made it seven. Mrs Goddard and Mrs Macreedy were talking with some enthusiasm about the Top Ten, and as soon as they saw me, they both said I should try it.

'The Top Ten Diet,' said Mrs Macreedy, when it became obvious I didn't have a clue what they were talking about. 'It's the only diet that's any good.'

'You don't believe there might be others?' I asked. 'There seems to be a different one in the papers every day. And the bookshops are full of them. Anything with Diet in the title sells millions. I might try it myself sometime.'

'How could they all work?' said Mrs Macreedy. 'It's obvious there must be one that's right.'

'Right for you, or right for everybody?' I mused, thinking I'd had this conversation before, only probably with a Mormon.

'Anyway,' I said, 'tell me about the Top Ten Diet. I'm all ears.'

'Quite a bit of you is tummy,' Mrs Macreedy pointed out, painfully with a pencil. 'But the Top Ten Diet is simplicity itself. You make a list of your ten favourite foods, and then you don't eat them. Ever.'

'Seems a bit harsh,' I thought out loud. 'What about curry? Do I list chicken korma, lamb dopi-aza, chicken dansak, sag aloo?'

'Oh no,' Mrs Goddard explained, 'You just put "curry", and then there's nine other things you can put on your list as well.'

That did it for me. All through the meeting, they were making lists of reasons why Cheeving was no place for a supermarket, and I was making a mental list of my favourite food.

Once the hall clock said a quarter to, and it was clear that nobody else was coming, we made a start.

I had been appointed as scribe, because I'd brought a notebook along, and they all sat looking at me, so it seemed I was chairman, too. Mrs General had dug out an old map of the village, which with a few pencil additions could pass for an up-to-date one. This was stuck to the wall with blue sticky stuff, right over the little notice asking people not to, but as the little notice was itself stuck to the wall with blue sticky stuff, we thought it would probably be all right. The outline of the supermarket had been drawn in with red pen, and it became clear that the whole village would be like a suburb of Saneways if the plan went ahead. On the table we were sitting around were copies of the same plans I'd seen in Huffleigh last week. My poor little tracings were completely upstaged. This was the real thing.

'It'll change the whole place,' said Mrs General. 'It won't be our village any more.'

I wrote 'Erosion of Village Character'.

'And it'll look horrible,' Mrs Goddard said.

I wrote 'Detrimental to Visual Amenity'.

'Is that what I said?' asked Mrs Goddard.

'It's what you meant,' I said. 'Planners have their own language.'

'Mind you,' said Mrs Goddard, 'those Hell's Angels up at Vineyard Cottage are detrimental to what you said.'

'Roaring up and down the street on their motorbikes,' added Mrs General. 'Some nights I have to turn up Black Sabbath really loud so I can hear what Ozzy's singing about.' We sat a moment, trying to digest that little snippet.

'Right,' said John Norman, who is at least the third generation of Normans to run the butcher's shop in the village, 'talking of traffic up the High Street, what's planning language for it will generate increased traffic flows up the High Street?'

'That's it in any language,' I said, and wrote it down.

John slaughters on the premises, and one morning a trailer was unloading half a dozen stout lambs, which were led around the back to the little pen where they would spend a few days before the chop. Or the leg, or half shoulder, or whatever. A small boy on his way to school asked, 'Where are those lambs going, Mummy?' and she said, 'To see Uncle John.' And the saying caught on, so here in the village nothing ever dies, but goes to see Uncle John.

The list grew. Even when I'd crossed out fish and chips and full English breakfast, there was still an impressive number of good reasons why any right-minded person would be horrified at the thought of Saneways building in Ted's old field. Personally, I'd contributed its effect on the church, spoiling its peaceful setting, and if the supermarket was going to be open on Sundays, luring the congregation away from worship.

Mrs General suggested a petition, and said we could have a copy in the Stores for people to sign. John said he would have one in the butcher's, and then they all looked at me, and I said all right, I'd put one in the church and remind people it was there when I gave out the notices. But I also stressed that everyone should write their own letter of objection, and encourage others to write, because a petition is easier to ignore than a whole bunch of letters.

Then we decided that our campaign should have a name. We were all too tired to discuss it, so we all agreed to the first suggestion that came up. Campaign Against the Supermarket in Cheeving.

'CATSIC,' said Mrs Macreedy. 'I like the sound of that.'

And then we called it a night.

As soon as I arrived home, I made out my own list.

1 Curry.
2 Fish and chips. I had a real crisis of conscience before putting this on, because if I'd been there when Jesus fed the five thousand, a couple of hundred of them would still be hungry.
3 Chilli con carne. I nearly included this under curry, but then I'd have had to think of something else to go on instead.
4 Full English breakfast. I only ever have this on holiday, when someone else is cooking, so it's a bit of a cheat, really.
5 Syrup sponge and custard.
6 Shepherd's pie.
7 Stew and dumplings.
8 Apple pie.
9 Lemon meringue pie. I once ate one the size of a Kinks LP, single-handed.
10 Sausage and mash.

☆ Number 4 ☆

I showed it to Hilary. She said thank you, because she was stuck for next week's menus. It was all very well for the boys, because they would eat anything, and if she asked them what they would like, that's exactly what they said. Anything. If *they'd* been at the feeding of the five thousand, a couple of thousand would have gone without. I stopped her, and said no, this is the Top Ten Diet, where you list all your favourite things and then don't eat them.

'So what do the rest of us eat?' she asked. 'While you're not eating any of this, are you going to watch while we do? And if you're not going to eat any of this, what *are* you going to eat?'

That was a bit of a poser, I had to admit. Hilary said, 'Why don't you go all the way, and just make a list of the things you don't like, and eat them? Go on the offal diet! Tripe, liver . . . '

I winced at the thought of it. It sounded too much like a dietary hair shirt. Then she said, 'You never knew my gran, did you?' Hilary's grandmother had died before we met. 'She firmly believed that anything you enjoyed must be sinful, and basically you could do anything you liked on the Sabbath, provided it wasn't work, and it wasn't fun. If Granddad ever said he liked what she was wearing, she'd never wear it again. She believed in plain cooking, too; she thought Oxo cubes were an exotic spice. She had the same attitude to food and religion.'

'Mrs Goddard and Mrs Macreedy both swear by it,' I said, a bit limply.

'All right for them,' snorted Hilary, 'neither of them has a family to worry about. They can make their way to the Celestial City without having to take anyone else along.'

It was late. God already has me down as that chap who falls asleep halfway through talking to him, and I didn't want to compound the felony. Hilary smiled sympathetically.

'Why don't you try the no crisps or chocolate biscuits diet?' she said. 'Or why not just accept you're cuddly?'

This was, I knew, a deliberate jibe.

'Never!' I said. 'Me, cuddly? I want a six-pack!'

Hilary raised one eyebrow. I wish I could raise one eyebrow. Then I could do sardonic like she does.

Chapter 5

A bite with me

Nothing much happens in Cheeving Halfpenny, although the little booklets we sell in the church tell a different story. Traditionally, in days gone by, the village had three main occupations: agriculture, poaching and smuggling. There are very few racy anecdotes about agriculture, the dashing deeds of men in smocks, but there are more about the poachers, who made Ferret's Bottom look like the Wild West. Most of the local stories are about the smugglers.

We may be thirty miles from the sea, as the gull flies, but Cheeving is just off the main road between Blicester and Huffleigh, and Goddling is only eleven miles north. The smugglers used the village as a central depot, and there are stories of gangs being pursued through the village by the revenue men, and the revenue men being pursued by the rest of the villagers because they tended to be on the side of those who served the cheapest drinks. The notorious Jacob Vulliger, who once smuggled a whole fleet of ships into Dorset disguised as a completely different fleet of ships, lived here for years under the guise of an honest innkeeper. As he is, apart from Mandy Hicks who was once on *Blind Date*,

Jacob Vulliger, smuggler

the only famous resident Cheeving has ever had, people are quite proud of him. This pride was not reflected at the Temporary Sign, where Arthur was holding forth to Paul Gruntle, the only other person there, about what he would do to smugglers, which is his word for anyone who goes to France to buy wine and beer instead of buying it from him at three times the price. He saw the possibility of a supermarket in the village as another nail in his coffin, and was blaming Paul for it, by association.

Outside the pub, at one of the wooden tables, shaded by an umbrella, a tramp was eating an enormous plateful of pie and chips, and drinking a pint of beer. He was a proper tramp, the sort tied together with string, old shoes burst on his feet, and ingrained grey dirt like charcoal on all his exposed surfaces. We get a lot of tramps through our village in the summer, so we're connoisseurs. This one scored at least eight point five on the vagrometer. He looked up with a contented grin as I went in, dabbing the corners of his mouth elegantly on his napkin, and then rather spoilt the effect with a belch that blew my hat off. I picked it up, removed the dog ends, and blessed him.

'Your pal Jason's outside,' said Arthur, pausing in his harangue for a moment, 'having his lunch.'

I brushed the worst of the dust off my hat and told him that the character actually eating lunch outside made Jason look like Orlando Bloom. Arthur ducked under the bar flap, looked outside, and said, 'Well, you could knock me down with a sledgehammer,' which was probably true. Then he lost interest, and carried on telling Paul why his father's decision to sell his field to Saneways had been a bad idea.

'They'll be doing six-packs and special offers and own brands, and spirits by the whole bottle,' he said. I said I thought that was the usual way to buy spirits, not that I ever do, and he looked at me as if I'd blasphemed. He pointed over his shoulder to the row of optics.

'That's the way to buy spirits,' he said firmly, 'and if you aren't concerned, Vicar, you ought to be, because a supermarket will cause underage drinking, to say nothing of Sunday opening.'

Without asking me what I wanted, he pulled me a pint of Busticles, and without asking what he wanted, I gave him some money, and took the stool next to Paul.

Ted Gruntle's son was a farmer through and

Sheep with the dumbles

through. As a child he had slept with a toy tractor, had wellies before he could even walk, and thought equipment catalogues were picture books. He was still in his overalls, propping up the bar, with a half-empty pint in front of him. I could tell it was half empty, not half full, because his face was as long as Ravel's *Bolero* and he was clearly not a happy man. There was obviously more on his mind than Arthur giving him an earbashing about the sale of the field.

I asked him what was up, because vicars have to, and he said there was an outbreak of the dumbles among the sheep, so if I was coming to the farm I'd have to wear wellingtons, because if you dip your feet wearing ordinary shoes, they fall off. Your shoes, that is, not your actual feet. I sympathized, because I'd seen sheep with the dumbles before. But I guessed there was something else troubling him, and asked.

He said angrily, 'Karen. My sister's back!'

I'd almost forgotten he had a sister. Karen had left school after A levels, which was unusual in itself, as most of the children from the old village families don't do A levels at all. It's a tradition in Cheeving Halfpenny that you leave school without qualifications, and then grumble because there are no jobs. A levels are for the middle classes, the people who move into the village from outside because they want a lifestyle instead of a life. But Karen was bright, and had done well. Then she had gone off to do a gap year, which had become two years, and Ted hadn't mentioned her for a long time. I'd even managed to forget her name until Paul said it.

'Back from where?' I asked. 'Where's she been?'

'India, would you believe?' said Paul. 'Two years ago she went off with her friend Janice, because she hadn't decided what she wanted to do at university, and wanted to see the world. A letter or a phone call wouldn't have killed her, but we heard nothing. We knew they'd got to India, because Janice came back, and told us Karen says not to worry, she's all right. Why didn't she tell us herself?'

He took a drink of beer, so I did the same.

'Do you know, Vicar, every day, Dad runs to the door when the post comes in case there's something from Karen? He doesn't say anything, but she's put years on him. And now she just turns up, and she's got a baby.'

'That is a turn up,' I agreed. 'Any sign of a husband? Partner?'

'You're kidding,' said Paul. 'And she won't be

called Karen, she says she's Shanti now, and the baby's called Dilip. Sounds like a misprint.'

'How's Ted taken it?' I asked.

'He's like a monkey with two tails,' said Paul. 'He won't ask questions, or tell her off, he thinks the baby's the bee's knees, and expects me to join in as if I was as happy as him.'

'Aren't you?' I asked him. 'Weren't you worried about her, too?'

'Of course I was! That's the point. She's got no idea how much she's hurt us, or what she's put us through, and she hasn't even said she's sorry!'

'I guess it will take Ted's mind off the supermarket business,' I said.

'Oh, that,' said Paul. Arthur was at the other end of the bar, polishing the peanuts. 'Selling that field was just common sense. Dad's already talking about buying another one our side of the road, so all the land will be together, now. That field was always out of the way.'

'A lot of people aren't happy that he sold it to Saneways,' I said. 'People don't all like change.'

Just then, a middle-aged man came in, and there would have been nothing unusual about him, except he was wearing a straw hat around his neck like a collar, with the top sticking up behind his head like the nimbus on a stained-glass saint.

'Yes, sir,' said Arthur, pretending he hadn't noticed, 'what can I get you.' The way Arthur says it, it isn't a question.

'I need something short,' said the man.

'Stand up, Toby,' called Arthur, to where Toby Chunt was sitting at a corner table, half hidden behind half a pint of Busticles. Toby slid forward on his chair until his feet touched the floor, and straightened up, but his glass was still taller than he was.

'A whisky,' said the man. 'A double.'

I couldn't resist it any longer.

'What happened to you?' I asked. 'I'm the Vicar – you can tell me in confidence.' Every ear in the bar strained to hear him say, 'I tried to collect the rent from Vineyard Cottage,' he said. 'For that Major Stern.'

'Ah,' we all said, as understanding dawned.

'All I got was a lot of abuse, language you wouldn't want your mother to hear, and they did this.' He fingered the brim of his hat sadly. Arthur, in a moment of compassion, produced his Swiss Army knife, withdrew the special blade for cutting the brims off straw hats, and freed our new friend so he could get his glass to his mouth. After all, he was hardly likely to buy another until he'd finished the first, and a customer buying doubles at lunch-time was a boon and a blessing.

'I think they've worked out,' I explained, 'that not paying rent leaves them more money for cigarettes, beer and works of Christian charity. OK,' I added as he raised a sceptical eyebrow, 'maybe not the Christian charity.'

'Well, it isn't my problem any more,' he said. 'Now the Major is going to have them . . . *evicted*.' The pause was supposed to be impressive, but we were all thinking it would be easier to pull a camel through the hole in a mint than get the squatters out of Vineyard Cottage.

Outside, the tramp had gone. The plate was spotless. This was a man who really appreciated his food, when he could get it. But how had he got it? It seemed unlikely that he could have overpowered Jason and stolen his lunch, but what other explanation could there be?

I stopped off at the butcher's because Hilary asked me to, and I always do what Hilary asks me to. A pound of mince. John sealed it in its plastic bag, passed it over the counter, and stood there expectantly.

'That's all, thanks,' I said.

'That's all?' John echoed. 'You mean I don't close for lunch, I put on my friendly welcoming-the-customer face, and go through the whole thing they teach us at butcher college and all you want is a pound of mince? What diet are you on?'

'The Top Ten Diet,' I told him. 'But only since last night,' I added, in case he was wondering why it wasn't working.

He snorted. 'So you don't even like mince, is that it?'

He obviously knew all about it. His business was probably suffering from it. I told him the mince was going to be Idiot Stew, and I was cooking it, and it's called Idiot Stew because you just chuck everything you've got in the fridge in it (except cheese) and nothing, *nothing* can go wrong. At the very worst, it tastes of Oxo.

'What with people on faddy diets, Veggie Vera picketing the shop every Saturday, and now a supermarket in the village, I'll be in the gutter soon,' John grumbled. He almost snatched my money, and handed over my change with great reluctance.

'The poster in the shop window probably doesn't help,' I suggested.

'What's wrong with it?' he asked.

'I think maybe people see the word CATSIC in a butcher's window, and don't read any further,' I said. 'Trust me on this.'

I told him about the dumbles at Gruntle's Farm, and he brightened a little.

'That means I can put the price of lamb up a bit,' he said.

'Do you get your lamb from Ted?' I asked.

'No,' he said, 'but even so. Business is business. It's an ill wind…'

After lunch, I decided to be the Rector of Pighill. I am Vicar of Cheeving Halfpenny and Rector of Pighill, a subtle difference that the people of the smaller parish hold on to, because it reinforces their belief that the outside world is Nothing To Do With Them. So I drove towards Blicester, then took the track off the main road, which goes to the village and then stops.

Beyond Pighill there is, according to the people who live there, nothing worth building a road to. I parked the car by St Ickinsect's, and stopped by the churchyard gate to admire the sheep. A small flock of impeccably reverent horned sheep is allowed to graze in the churchyard during the summer months. This saves a lot of effort and loss of life keeping it clear by more conventional means. On the gate is a notice which says: 'Warnen. Ship. Doan ee put flars on graves, as ship do it they flars.'

This is supposed to be amusing and whimsical, while at the same time pointing out the futility of putting flowers on graves.

The west window shows the story of St Ickinsect, who was a Saxon. As a baby, his pious parents noticed that when he lay in his crib rubbing his little legs together, he was actually playing *Lux aeterna*, and his first words were reputedly '*Dominus vobiscum*'. As he grew up, his talent for stridulation increased, and to this day, the monks of his Order wear corduroy trousers, and skilled devotees can walk around the cloister playing 'Father hear the prayer we offer' with their thighs.

Up in the roof, what looks like an ornate carved boss is actually a cushion, because Doris the Levitatrix would otherwise have banged her head when the ecstasy raised her. Really, it was put there when the church was largely rebuilt in 1875, because a church with no architectural merit needs all the legends it can get.

I went to see Isaac Stools first. Isaac is the last of the old farm labourers who were once the population of Pighill before all the solicitors, merchant bankers and brokers moved in. Isaac made me welcome, sat me down, and then started telling me that people in Cheeving were an ungrateful lot of blanks who didn't recognize a good thing when they saw it.

'If you don't want supermarket, tell 'em to come over here. We'll have it.'

Pighill has no pub, shop, post office or anything else much. Nor has it ever had. High on rustic charm, low on facilities. For hundreds of years it lay in its little valley, invisible from the main road, except for the church tower, and then only in winter when there are no leaves on the trees. People like Isaac rely on the weekly bus to Huffleigh to get any shopping at all, and they have to walk half a mile up the main road to catch it.

'We'd love a big shop here, walking distance,' said Isaac. 'All right for you, with your pub and your butcher's and your post office and your General Stores. You can afford to say no. Over here in Pighill, we'd say yes so loud you'd hear us in Blicester.'

I heard much the same thing at Mick Wells's.

'What's the news, Mick?' I asked. He looked puzzled.

'You mean the news on the wireless?' and I said no, the news in the village. He looked nonplussed, and sucked his teeth.

'No news here, Rector,' he said. 'That Mrs Baring had to back her car down the lane so the milk lorry could get to the farm.'

'Yes?' I prompted him, waiting for the punchline. There wasn't one. So I asked him what he thought about the possibility of a big shop in

Cheeving. It would be wasted on us, he said, they ought to build it where it would really be appreciated. He and Isaac were obviously as one on the subject, and again, later, over tea with Mrs Gunny, she expressed the same sentiments. I guessed that if it came to it, Pighill would be divided between those who had cars and could drive to the shops, who would certainly oppose any development in the village larger than a garden shed, because they always did; and those older people who needed the shops to come to them, because the bus fare was a sizeable addition to their weekly bill. It occurred to me that opposing the plan for Cheeving might have another effect; Saneways might look for an alternative site, where there were too few people for the objections to be loud enough to notice.

Leaving the village, I had to back halfway down the lane so the milk lorry could get to the farm. With so much excitement in one week, the people of Pighill would have a topic of conversation for a long time to come.

There was cricket that evening at Cheeving. Proper village cricket, fourteen eight-ball overs each way, so everyone goes out and slashes wildly at everything, every ball is hit as hard as is humanly possible, and that's before the match even starts. I read the boys their story, reassured them that it was all a long time ago and a long way off, and walked through the churchyard, through the field in question, to the cricket field, with a can of Busticles for the interval. The visitors were Bishops Wibbling, and ancient rivalries that pre-date the

Reformation always make this a good match.

But what immediately caught my eye was the sightscreen. Cheeving are a side that thinks white trousers are poncey, where they don't always have bails, and yet here was a sightscreen. Mark Hadlow, the captain, was just padding up on the steps of the hut that passes for a pavilion, and I asked him about the startling new piece of equipment.

'A gift,' he explained.

'Who loves us enough to give us a new sightscreen?' I asked. Mark pointed to the logo in the bottom right-hand corner. I thought it was the maker's mark, but when I looked, there was the unmistakable cross-eyed, tongue-waggling face of Sammy Saneway, the symbol of Saneways Supermarkets. First the children's badges, now the village cricket team.

'Saneways gave you an expensive bit of kit, just like that?'

'Part of their Caring for the Community scheme,' said Mark. 'If you'd been here on Saturday, we all had our photo taken in front of it for the *Blicester Bugle*, with the store manager from Huffleigh. They'd probably have asked you to bless it. Now I'm opening. Say one for me.'

And off he strode to the wicket, to open the batting with Jason. Jason is good enough to go in at number two, but it's as a bowler he really comes into his own. With his facial ornaments glittering in the low sunlight, his mullet blowing in the wind, and the smoke from his roll-up surrounding him with an almost supernatural aura, his tattoos take

on a life of their own, and he strikes terror into any batsman's heart. His run-up starts almost out of sight, and the batsman by this time is like a rabbit mesmerized by the headlights of a truck, trembling and incapable of any reasoned response. So we usually win.

The team were on good form, and the match was marred only by a mighty hit from one of the Bishops Wibbling openers being caught on the boundary by Lennox the Rottweiler, who crunched the ball like an apple. They claimed six, we claimed a catch, and the umpire gave a four to save noses being broken. There was a bit of a hunt for another ball, and the match continued. The evening concluded with a victory for the home team, and the whole lot of them trooped off down to the Temporary Sign to put right the damage that fresh air and exercise can do to a young man's constitution. And I made my way home wondering whether I'd misjudged Saneways, who seemed to have the interests of the village at heart after all.

Chapter 6

I saw three chips

The boys have discovered a whole new way of winding us up. They take it in turns to come into our bedroom in the small hours of the morning, shaking me awake and saying, 'Here I am, for you called me.' They then get sent back to bed with the instruction to stay there until our alarm goes off. If the Lord really did want to talk to them, I hope he would part the clouds unmistakably, and say, in his best Orson Welles tones, 'Tidy your room!'

So there I was at breakfast, feeling a little bit duntish for lack of sleep. When Hilary asked me what my plans for the day were, my instinct was to say I intended lacing their cocoa with Mogadon.

'What's a Mogadon?' they asked, coming into the kitchen, fresh as daisies and ready for school.

'An extinct North American mammal like a hairy elephant,' I said, proving how easy it is to lie once you get in practice.

'Why don't you just stop having sugar in your tea and coffee?' asked Hilary.

'What good would that do?' I replied. 'I need to turn my whole diet around, not just tinker with the details.' Not having sugar in tea is like not having tealeaves, as far as I'm concerned.

'How many cups do you have a day?' I thought about it. One first thing, one with breakfast, mid morning, lunchtime, teatime (of course), one after dinner, one during the evening, and then people I visit are always offering them during the day. More tea, Vicar, as they say.

'About six,' I answered, and there was a peal of thunder from the clear sky.

'So that's twelve spoonfuls of sugar,' she said. 'Do you know what that would look like, all at once?'

'But I hate tea without sugar,' I said. 'And coffee.'

'You hate just about everything you eat at the moment,' she said. I promised I'd give it a try.

The boys looked thoughtful. 'Where can you get tapeworms?' they asked.

'From eating badly cooked food, I think,' I answered, 'especially like pork.'

'No,' they said, 'where can you *get* them? Because Miss Jolly said if you have tapeworms you lose a lot of weight because they eat your food for you, and everybody wants to lose weight, don't they? Everybody in the village is talking about it. So we thought if we could get some tapeworms –'

Scale (Fathoms)

'Don't even think about it!' I said.

I saw three chips

Then I told Hilary that I didn't fancy the rest of
my bacon, and I would get some exercise by visiting
some of the outlying parts of the village, starting
with the Brigadier.

Brigadier Hollywood is over ninety, and has
spent the best part of his life in Africa – soldier,
explorer and white hunter. He's written half a shelf
of books about his travels and experiences, some
of them even true. The Hollywoods were once the
most distinguished family in the village, and they
have their own vault in St Gargoyle's. The Brigadier's ancestors sent generations of young soldiers
to their deaths from the safety of distant hills,
but the Brigadier's father broke with tradition by
serving with gallantry and distinction in the First
World War. The Brigadier himself was in Africa
in the thirties anyway, so taking time out from
potting at wildlife to see off a few Germans and
Italians was a natural move. The cottage he now
shares with Percy, his unmarried son, himself over
sixty and the last of the Hollywoods, is shabby,
and set a little apart from the rest of the village,
ideal for a vicar trying to burn a few calories. It's
a treasure trove of ethnic curios, full of trophies
and souvenirs. Leopard skins, in various stages of
mangy decay, adorn the walls as well as the floors.
Snake skins, whole snakes in bottles, elephants'
feet and stuffed crocodiles, drums and spears, pots,
beads and ghastly sculptures in black wood cram
every corner. Fantastically horned skulls make the
place a hazard for the unwary clergyman. As my
eyes became accustomed to the gloom of the tiny,

overcrowded rooms, it became apparent that the occasional table was a tribal drum, and that the very rug underfoot had claws and teeth.

The Brigadier has a way of beginning every other sentence, 'When I was in Africah . . .', and the social worker who once interrupted him with a curious 'Oh – were you in Africa?' reduced the old man to wide-eyed, incredulous silence. He hates social workers in any case. He sees them as a threat to his freedom. If part of the explanation for all the evil in the world is that God insists on leaving us free, then social workers, according to the Brigadier, represent Satan and all his works in spades.

My first Vicar told me, 'Look after your old people,' so I do. The Brigadier enjoys an audience for his stories, and I enjoy not having to listen to anything more exacting. The Brigadier has no problems, spiritual or material, is in excellent health, and on speaking terms with God, although he tended to think that God agreed with him, rather than the other way round. Then it was nearly

lunchtime, and if I stayed any longer I would be offered what the Brigadier usually calls 'a sniftah', so I said goodbye, and let him see me out, and walked back to the village.

Next to the one about CATSIC, Mrs General had a big notice in her window announcing that details of the General Diet were available inside. Intrigued, I went in and asked.

'You can eat anything you like,' said Mrs General, 'so long as you buy it here. That's why it's called the General Diet. If I sell it, it's all right, and if I don't, it isn't.'

I looked around. Like a lot of village shops, the General Store gets used as any port in a storm when we run out of something and don't want to drive to Huffleigh. John the Butcher is different. People come from miles around for his sausages, and even further for his fresh meat. But apart from one or two really old people, nobody much does *all* their shopping at the Stores. Food tins are dusty, if not actually rusty. Cornflake boxes don't necessarily rattle when you shake them. Vegetables look tired and listless. If you only ate what Mrs General sold, you would lose weight from sheer loss of appetite. Going on the General Diet would be like joining the Exclusive Brethren.

'It means shopping responsibly,' said Mrs General, 'and in particular, not buying anything from Saneways.'

'Have you had any takers yet?' I asked.

'Hard to tell,' she said. 'I don't know what people buy when they're not here. All I can do is sell them all I can, and trust them.'

It began to fall into place. This was not really a diet, but a bit of political ideology wearing a diet's hat. I bought a torch battery I didn't need, just to be polite.

Outside the Stores, Mrs Pershore was raising her voice to Mrs Macreedy. Being curious (I think the word we're after here is 'nosy'), I studied the post-cards in the window so that I could listen. Gripping stuff, what with a ladies' bike being for sale, a baby buggy, and as much manure and firewood as you could want, a babysitter being available, a lost cat, and yoga at the Hall on Thursdays. Who says Cheeving is a sleepy backwater? But I was more interested in the animated conversation going on a few feet away. I gathered that Mrs Macreedy had at some time in the past been given a first-class stamp by Mrs Pershore, and now Mrs Pershore was demanding her stamp back, or at least one just like it, and Mrs Macreedy said she didn't have one, and Mrs Pershore was saying that was just typical, she didn't have one the last time so she borrowed one of Mrs Pershore's. At this point I couldn't stand it any more, opened my wallet, and gave Mrs Pershore a stamp. She stuck it on her letter and posted it, and then said to Mrs Macreedy, 'But that's still one you owe me!'

'No,' I said, 'I've just given you the one she owed you, so now if she owes anyone a stamp, it's me.'

'A debt's a debt,' said Mrs Pershore. It isn't just the corners of her mouth that turn down, it's her whole face.

'Have you told Mrs General that?' I asked. 'Did you tell her not to cancel what you owed her?'

I would like to be able to say that Mrs Pershore was suitably chastened and humbled, and apologized profusely to me and Mrs Macreedy. But I can't, because she didn't. She sniffed a monumental sniff that sucked the knot on her headscarf up her nose, and stalked off down the High Street.

'She's a one,' said Mrs Macreedy.

'Good job too,' I said. 'I'd hate to think there were any more of her.'

'I owe you a stamp,' she said.

'No, you don't,' I said. It made me sad that she'd even said it.

By now I thought my reputation for eating with publicans and sinners needed enhancing, so seeing Lennox the Rottweiler outside the Temporary Sign chewing what looked like a postman's leg, or at least somebody's leg in a blue serge trouser, I joined

Jason inside for a bag of ready salted, and a pint of Busticles.

'I was reading the Bible this morning,' he said, not caring whether anyone heard him or not, which is a healthy sign. 'Did you know Jesus had four brothers?'

'Yes,' I said. 'A lot of people don't like that, because they think it reflects badly on Mary and Joseph.'

'I wasn't pleased because I want to be more like him, so I wanted him to be an only child.'

'You're not an only child,' I said.

'Yes I am,' he said, 'and so is my brother.'

Ferret's Bottom is one of those places where only having one child would have been a sign of weakness in days gone by. The feud between the Orrells and the Bloats, the origin of which is lost in the mists of iniquity, relied on large families growing up and outnumbering the opposition. I started explaining that not being an only child made Jesus more like him, but Jason changed the subject abruptly.

'What you want, Vicar,' he said, helping himself to my crisps, 'is more of those modern hymns – the sort you get on *Songs of Praise*.'

'You watch *Songs of Praise*?' I know he's become a Christian, but even so . . .

'No need to go spreading it around,' he said. 'Reading the Bible's all right, because people get killed, but I still got my reputation.'

'Anyway,' I said, 'I know what I'd like, but it's Dennis who plays the organ, and he always says "The choir won't sing that, Vicar", if I suggest anything written since the war.'

'And the services sometimes go over my head,' admitted Jason. 'I can't be doing with all them eths.'

'Eths?'

'You know – eateth, drinketh, sinneth.'

I nodded agreement. 'Trouble is,' I said, 'a lot of people grew up with that, and for years the 1662 Prayer Book was all there was. They're used to it. Mind you, I bet there's some who think 1662 is too trendy, and they want 1549, so I could pray against the Bishop of Rome and his detestable enormities.'

'I saw them once,' said Jason, 'playing in a club in Blicester. They were loud.'

David Mortimer, a solicitor with Pules, Mortimer and Nutleg, had been drinking by himself at a table, but now he came over to the bar. He's a Roman Catholic, but we usually get on, as long as there are no matches around. He's a bit too smooth and silky for my liking, and he stands too close to you when he speaks. He looked at the little blackboard propped on the bar, and asked Arthur, 'Is the skate pan-fried?'

'As opposed to what?' asked Arthur. 'Dustbin-lid fried? Coal-shovel fried?'

'Is it in batter?' asked David, patiently. Arthur said yes, it was, and very nice batter it was, too. David looked at the board again, and said he'd have the chicken. Arthur pushed open the kitchen door and shouted, 'One chicken in batter!'

Arthur may not be the source of all evil, as some people say, but he certainly does his bit. David Mortimer turned to me, so I wiped that silly grin off my face.

'Excuse me, Vicar,' he said, standing too close (told you!), 'but I couldn't help overhearing your conversation.'

'I'm sorry,' I said. 'We'll keep it down.'

'No, no,' he said. 'I agree with you entirely. Some of our people still hanker after Latin. They can't understand a word, but they grew up with it.' Jason hudged his stool along, to make room for David. I noticed he took my crisps with him.

'This whole village is the same,' David went on. 'Some people think it should never change, or grow. But it's like the church. If it isn't changing and growing, it's dying.'

'True,' I said. 'If anybody wants to build a conservatory, or put in double glazing, half a dozen others will object, just because.'

'Do you think the two are linked?' asked David. 'If the village was more forward-looking, might the church be more amenable to progress? You might get them singing "Shine, Jesus shine" yet.'

'I'd be pleased if I could get them singing "Tell out, my soul",' I told him.

'Fine,' said David. 'So will we see you on Thursday?'

'Thursday?'

'Some of us are having a meeting here, to discuss the proposed development. There's been a lot of adverse comment and bad publicity, and we feel some of the positive aspects could do with emphasizing. Here at eight o'clock.'

'Here?' I said. 'What will Arthur say? He's against the whole thing.'

'He was,' said David, 'but now he sees a supermarket will bring visitors, maybe more houses even, and visitors mean trade. A shopping trip and lunch at a country pub. Sounds good to me. Eight o'clock on Thursday.'

'Will you go?' asked Jason when David had gone, leaving a faint silvery trail on the pub carpet behind him.

'I might,' I said, 'just to hear what's said. But I don't like the idea of more houses.'

'Not even if the new people are Christians?' Jason said. 'Christians who might like to sing new songs and wave their arms about?'

'The last time you waved your arms about,' I reminded him, 'you tipped lager all over Mrs Hopkins. She wasn't best pleased.'

'Only because when she got home, her old man thought it was a new perfume and molested her,' he said.

He was right. Charisma can make your lunch late.

Chapter 7

Away in a mangetout

It was two o'clock on Thursday. It was the day my watch strap broke, and the day Wilkins phoned to tell me he'd come back from his holiday in Latvia and found his curate had swapped the church for five magic beans. That's the trouble with being single – you can't share your troubles over supper, and have to call your friends. I was just adjusting my expenses claim – how I hate that word 'fiddling' – when I had to answer the door, and was quite surprised to see Mrs Brewer on the doorstep. Mrs Brewer hasn't really spoken to me since we were in the butcher's a year ago, and the boys said, 'You've got a funny name.'

'Brewer's not a funny name,' she said, with one of those looks that suggest children shouldn't even be seen, let alone heard.

'No, your first name,' they said. 'Bootface.'

Mrs Brewer sniffed so hard several people in the shop passed out for lack of oxygen. I wished the tiles on the floor would open up and swallow me, and that the boys wouldn't take everything I said literally. I asked the good lady in, decided this was one for the kitchen rather than the study, and led her through. I offered her coffee, but she shook her head.

'I'm that angry, Vicar,' she said, 'I had to tell someone.'

'It's what I'm here for,' I said. 'This doesn't have anything to do with magic beans, does it?'

Mrs Brewer gave me a withering look. No wonder I look older than I am.

'That Jim Donovan!' she said.

Jim Donovan, he of the pink Cadillac, is Big Jim to most of us. Mrs Brewer spends her weekday mornings doing his housework, and cooks his lunch. Lunch has to be over by two, because Wall Street opens, and whatever else that means, it means Jim has eyes only for his computer monitor. On Saturday and Sunday, Jim has lunch in the pub, and Myrtle goes in and makes his bed and tidies things up.

'I asked Jim Donovan for a rise,' she said. 'He's been paying me the same since I started, and I do his food shopping, and I do *not* skimp on his lunch,' she emphasized, as if anyone had suggested she might. I nodded vaguely, wishing she'd get to the point.

'He said, "How much would you like?" and I said ten pounds would be nice. And do you know what he said, Vicar?'

'I wasn't there,' I reminded her.

'He said, "Call it fifteen."'

'That's nice,' I said. 'You ask for ten, and he offers you fifteen. But you're angry?'

'That daft Myrtle, who only comes in weekends, and he has to stand over her while she makes a cup of tea, he said, "I'll do the same for Myrtle."'

'So she gets a rise, too,' I said. 'That sounds all right.'

'Trust you to take her part,' she said. 'It isn't right, giving her the same as me. I'm getting three pounds a day extra, and she's getting seven pounds fifty. Is that fair?'

Whenever the boys say something isn't fair, I ask them to show me where it says it has to be fair. I wanted to say the same to Mrs Brewer, but I was actually pleased that she was talking to me at all, so instead I asked her where she stood in the Great Supermarket Debate, just to keep the conversation going.

'I'm all in favour,' she said. 'I don't want to be trailing over to Huffleigh to get Jim's shopping twice a week.'

'But you use the butcher's here,' I reminded her, a bit embarrassed.

'For me and John, yes,' she said, 'but I get all Jim's stuff in Saneways. It's cheaper.'

'I see,' I said. 'You get your meat here, because it's better, and Jim's at Saneways because it's cheaper.'

'And if they open a shop here, it'll be cheaper still, because I won't be using the petrol,' she said.

'I suppose Jim can pay who he likes what he likes,' I said. 'It's his money.'

'That's as maybe,' said Mrs Brewer, 'but that Myrtle doesn't deserve it.'

'If we all got what we deserved,' I said, 'there'd be a lot more kicks up a lot more backsides.'

'Will you speak to him?' she said.

'I always speak to him,' I said.

'About the money?' she prompted.

'Not my problem,' I said. 'And not yours, really.'

Another satisfied customer, I thought, as she stomped off down the drive.

A quick call in at the General Stores was called for, to replenish the Vicarage stocks of cheese, and to see how the CATSIC petition was developing. Mrs General held out the clipboard with a thick layer of papers gripped to it.

'I used the shop calculator,' she said, 'to work out the figures and percentages.'

I was impressed. The shop calculator is huge, full of wheels, and burns coke.

'Of people asked,' she explained, 'twenty-five per cent refused to sign at all, twenty per cent said they would sign, but then didn't, and twelve per cent signed and then thought better of it and made me take them off again.'

'Would that be the cricket team?' I asked.

Mrs General checked her papers, and nodded. 'And forty three per cent actually signed,' she said proudly.

'Actually,' I said, looking down the names, 'the forty-three per cent who signed all seem to have signed several times. There's more names here than there are people in the village.'

'That shows, though, doesn't it,' said Mrs General, 'that the people who feel strongly feel *really* strongly. Nothing lukewarm about this lot.'

'There's a sermon there, somewhere,' I said. ' But

on the other hand, I notice that both Mickey *and* Minnie Mouse have signed, and all the Simpson family from Springfield, including Maggie, who can't even speak, let alone write.'

'There may be a bit of poetic licence there,' Mrs General said, blushing slightly.

'We can't hand this in to the Planning Committee like this,' I insisted. 'We've got to get more real people to sign it. And if most people won't, then maybe we have to accept that they really do want a socking great supermarket looming over the church.'

I chose my cheese with care. Mrs General keeps two sorts of cheese. There is Mild Cheddar, and Strong Cheddar. Even this she thinks is spoiling us, and pandering to the citified whims of the incomers. I opted for the Strong Cheddar, on the grounds that it tastes faintly cheesy.

And then on down the village to the workshops, for a new watch strap. I say nothing much happens in Cheeving Halfpenny, but it must have done once, a few years before I arrived. A farmhouse was converted into workshop units. It had been two good-sized properties, and the stables and barn were just about to become the sort of picturesque ruin they make jigsaws of, when somebody not only had a better idea, they did something about it. They must have done it in winter, because the swallows and martins and swifts came back to what had been their farmyard, and moved in as if nothing had changed. There are eight workshops around a courtyard, a mixture of whatever activities can be done in the space of one large room, and they don't do anything twee or arty. One of them makes leather belts, another posthumously stuffs small mammals. Grace and her sister make pies, and Tony fixes clocks and watches.

Already there when I arrived was Gordon, with his watch. The hands were keeping good enough time, but the face was spinning around. Gordon never caught it doing it, just every time he looked, the 12 was somewhere different.

Tony looked at it, and said, 'Leave it with me.'

Gordon said yes, but was there any chance of a courtesy watch, one he could borrow until this one was fixed? Tony rummaged, and handed him a digital, the sort garages used to almost give away with petrol. Gordon picked it up as if it was a lizard. He feels the same way about *Common Worship*, or anything that isn't the Book of Common Prayer, and CDs.

Gordon has the largest record collection in the county. Nothing is much later than 1963. If cool was terminal, Gordon would be immortal. He hunts around jumble sales and boot fairs, and the likes of Alma Cogan, David Whitfield and Dennis Lotis are his favourites, although he also has a soft spot for those LPs that ask 'Can YOU tell the difference between these and the original recordings?' As the original recordings are now long forgotten, the answer is probably 'No', but at the time it would have been 'Are you serious?' The very mention of CDs to Gordon brings forth scorn and sarcasm. They are a passing craze, and fit only for hanging up to scare birds off your broad beans. Vinyl is the real thing. Gordon says he will buy a CD player if They promise, in writing, not to invent anything else.

Gordon can lower the turnout at any function by providing the music. Once he offered to raise funds with a twenty-four-hour discathon at the Village Hall. He thought people would come and pay to have their requests played, but in fact nobody actually wanted to hear anything he had. But rumour had it he sat for a whole Saturday afternoon, and through the night, and right up to Sunday lunchtime, playing records to an empty hall, and announcing the titles, too. Afterwards, he took umbrage, and refused to say who might have benefited from the funds he didn't raise, with the implication that everyone lost out, from the Scouts to St Gargoyle's.

When he saw the digital watch, his technophobia kicked in. The watch said 15.48, and Gordon has never recognized any such time. Around ten to four, his own watch would have said, and he would have understood. Like 'Forgive us our sins'. I know what that means, and so do you, but there are plenty of people, especially over at Pighill, who prefer the original, because somehow, admitting to trespass seems less serious.

'I can't use this,' said Gordon.

'Course you can,' said Tony. 'It's only until tomorrow.'

But we could see Gordon's rising panic. Tony was afraid he might have to slap him, and the thought of everyone buying him drinks was embarrassing. So he handed Gordon his old watch back. Gordon looked at it afresh, screwing up his eyes just enough so he could see the hands, but not read the numbers, and walked out under the wheeling swallows.

'I meant to ask him whether he'd sign the petition at the Stores,' I said, as Tony clipped a new strap onto my watch. 'Do you think he'd be against a huge great supermarket looming over the village?'

'Hard one, that,' said Tony.

After supper that evening, which had cheese in it, I had the perfect excuse to skive out of the washing up, because Jason and Melony came to talk about the plans for their wedding, which was only a few weeks away. We managed to manoeuvre Melony, whose generous superstructure was a hazard to fragile ornaments, flower arrangements and pot plants, into the study without too much loss and breakage. It's important to keep Melony moving in straight lines. Sudden changes of direction could clear a shelf of books. When God was giving out busts, Melony went round at least twice, like a vicar at a buffet.

I try to help couples prepare, not just for a wedding, which lasts an afternoon, but for a marriage, which lasts longer, usually. When we were settled comfortably, I asked Jason, 'What's the most annoying thing about Melony?'

He thought about it while he rolled a cigarette like a cocktail stick. 'She keeps wanting me to be tidy,' he said. 'And I think I'm a natural scruff.'

There followed a lively discussion about whether it was possible, if you were a person who puts things away, to live with someone who leaves things about. I said I lived with two of them, who made Jason seem like a filing clerk by comparison. I'm quite used to the feeling of treading on a Lego brick in the middle of the night. Then I asked Melony what was the most annoying thing about Jason. She didn't have to think about it.

'It isn't just he's untidy,' she said. 'He loses things. He came home in his socks a little while ago, because he'd lost his new trainers. How can you *lose* new trainers?'

Jason looked suitably embarrassed. I changed the subject.

We'd already been through the various forms of service, and decided against the one that had the bit about 'brute beasts which have no understanding' in it, but also decided against a modern language service. Jason did, after all, come from Ferret's Bottom, where colour TV is still regarded with suspicion. Now we were going to talk about hymns, and the details of the service, the things that would make it personal and memorable for them. I told them I would call the banns for the first time at the morning service on Sunday. Hilary brought us coffee, and we settled down to browse through hymn books.

We made the usual jokes about 'Fight the good fight' and 'Through the night of doubt and sorrow'. As gently as I could, I explained to Melony that the song from *Titanic* wasn't a hymn, and neither was 'Unchained Melody'. And anything that had to be rapped, not sung, was out of the question. But Sunday by Sunday, Jason had been hearing more and more hymns, and in his enthusiasm, he was hard pressed to find any that weren't his favourites.

'Can we have "Morning has broken"?' he asked.

'You can,' I assured him. 'Dennis will turn up his nose, but he'll play it, because he's a pro.'

We spent so much time discussing the other hymns that Jason wearily suggested we sang 'Morning has broken' three times. Finally, I gave them a hymn book to take away, because I had to keep a promise at the pub.

'Ah, Vicar,' said David Mortimer, standing up as I went in, 'let me get you a drink.'

The bar was empty except for a small group of people sitting around the table just inside the door, because there was football on TV, and the Temporary Sign doesn't have one. I thanked him, and asked for a pint of Busticles.

'Good,' said David, winking at the others, 'a man of the people.'

But I noticed the others were drinking wine. Arthur pulled my pint, came round from behind the bar, and pulled a chair up to the table.

'We were just saying,' said David, by way of bringing me up to date, 'that this new development could be good news for the whole village. Jobs for local people, more people coming here, putting us on the map.'

I liked the 'us'. David was what most people in Cheeving would have called an incomer. Mind you, there were people who had lived in the village since childhood who were still regarded as incomers. It all depended how you fitted in. If you shop at the local shops and follow the local customs, like eating mushrooms on Dry Pants Friday, at least people can see you've made an effort. I looked around the table, at the pro-supermarket lobby. Charlie Dodds is the farmer, Ted Gruntle's neighbour, who owns most of the land around the church, adjoining the supermarket site. Andy Lefevre is a builder. David Mortimer is a solicitor. A picture began to emerge.

'And with a big retail store here,' David went on, 'the need for further development will be easy to sell to the District Council.'

'Haven't the planners drawn a sort of line around the village?' I asked. 'The famous Planning Envelope?'

'The village can't stay the same for ever,' said Arthur.

'I thought you were against the whole thing,' I said to him.

'What sort of church would you rather be Vicar of?' he asked. 'A little country parish with a couple of dozen regulars, or a big one with hundreds of people all singing and clapping? Who would you rather preach to? The faithful few, or a full house? This pub could become a goldmine.'

The others nodded their assent. They could all see the possibility of making a great deal of money out of what everyone else would see as the village being swallowed up by development.

'I shouldn't be here,' I decided out loud. It goes against the grain to leave a full pint, but I stood up.

'Typical,' said David. 'People say, "What can we do to help this village come into the twenty-first century?" And when something good comes along, they reject it, and say, "*Apart* from that, what can we do to help this village?" You know you could *fill* your church, Vicar, with modern hymns, PowerPoint graphics, a proper kitchen – a loo, even. But no. Let's just carry on the same old way, because we don't want to upset the oldies.'

I felt sad walking back up the street. I passed Henry Dolt, the undertaker, going the other way.

'Evening Henry,' I said. 'How's business?'

'Terrible,' he said. 'If it doesn't improve, I'm going to kill somebody.'

'Penny for them,' said Hilary later, as we sat up in bed. She noticed I hadn't turned the page of *What Cassock?* for several minutes.

'I was thinking about the supermarket,' I said. 'And the more I think about it, the more I'm against it. The people who want it aren't concerned about the village, or ordinary people, just about lining their own pockets.'

'Does that make it a bad thing?' she asked. 'Just because the people that want it have all the wrong motives, does that make it wrong?'

'That's ethics, isn't it? I stopped doing ethics when I left college.'

Hilary put down her magazine and moved closer to me. 'Do you want to?' she asked.

I did, and said so. The door opened. It was one of the boys.

'Here I am,' he said brightly, 'for you called me!'

Chapter 8

Cod moves in a mysterious way

Breakfast was a sombre affair until I read the paper. There was nothing breakfasty in my Top Ten, so I could have what I liked, but it felt like duty rather than pleasure, like filling the car with petrol. I was getting fed up with eating things I didn't particularly enjoy, and having actual withdrawal symptoms because I wasn't getting any curry, which makes my handwriting go spidery. I was beginning to think that the Top Ten Diet was flying in the face of human nature, because the whole point of food is surely that you have to enjoy it. Meals are more than pit stops, and telling someone they can't do something, or eat something, is the surest way to make them want to do it, or eat it. Reducing my diet to a list of Thou Shalt Nots was making me unhappy, and driving Hilary to distraction. It's true, I had that smug virtuous feeling you get when you don't have a drink because you're driving, and/or you don't kick someone on the bum even though they're an open target and they deserve it, but that didn't compensate for all the good food I wasn't getting. So when I read about the Twenty-Six Day Alphabet

Diet I was intrigued and
encouraged. Not eating
my Top Ten foods
hadn't, in any case,
made any
appreciable
difference
to my
weight or
my
waistline.

There in
the paper, in
the section they call *Me*, was a nice smiley model
who looked as if she hadn't eaten anything, ever,
and underneath were the details. On the first day,
you only ate food beginning with A, which was fine
if you like avocados and asparagus. On the second
day, you could have bacon and beans and bread,
and on the third day, joy! Curry!

'What happens when you get to X?' asked
Hilary.

'You can have as many as you like,' I said. 'Boiled,
fried, or scrambled.'

'We can think of lots of food beginning with A,'
said the boys.

'Go on,' I said.

'A Mars bar. A chip. A hamburger. A fish finger.'

'That would be cheating,' I said, sternly. They
looked suitably chastened, and lapsed into a
private conversation about bornflakes, bausages
and bocolate.

'Does this mean you can go back to eating things you like?' asked Hilary. 'Is the Top Ten Diet consigned to history with the hula hoop, the spacehopper, and Rubik's cube?'

'Rubik's cube will be consigned to history when I can do it,' I said.

'And I thought those creaking noises in your study were your knees flexing when you pray,' she said. And then something occurred to her. 'This Top Ten Diet,' she said. 'Where did you say you heard about it?'

'It was Mrs Macreedy and Mrs Goddard,' I said.

'Which ones? The Mrs Macreedy who almost disappears sideways on? The Mrs Goddard who has to run about in the shower to get wet?'

Her irony wasn't wasted on me. The two ladies in question are both, how can we put it? Stout. On reflection, neither of them gave the impression they were on any diet at all, and definitely not one that actually worked. But I was still on the defensive. None of us is very good at letting go of a belief, no matter how daft it is. I said, 'Mrs Goddard swears by it.'

Hilary grinned. 'The lady doth protein too much, methinks,' she said. 'So what do you want for lunch?'

I thought about what the boys had said. A cornish pasty. A bacon sandwich. But then I stiffened the blood, summoned up the sinews, and decided. 'Apples.'

The telephone rang. If I'm lucky, I can have breakfast and say my morning prayers without the telephone interrupting. Early calls sometimes mean someone has died in the night and Henry Dolt rings as soon as he thinks I'll be up. But this was John the butcher, and it was good news.

'Good news!' he shouted, which was how I knew. 'The Planning Committee meeting was last night, and they turned it down. I was there!'

'Excellent,' I said. 'Nothing like a butcher with a straw hat and a big cleaver to put the frighteners on the local council.'

'They said it was too big, and too near the church. And the chairman criticized them for not showing the church on the plan. I'm going to phone Mrs General and the others.'

I tried to thank him, but found I was thanking nobody, because he'd put the phone down. I didn't have to tell Hilary what he'd said, because he's one of those people who doesn't really need a telephone at all, or not for local calls, anyway. He could stand outside his shop and shout.

I arranged the fridge magnets to read Genesis 45.18, and left the house whistling. The news had spread through the village like chickenpox through playschool. Banners fluttered in the breeze, the church bells rang out like the end of the 1812 Overture, flocks of pigeons wheeled madly, cheering crowds waved flags as confetti fell in great drifts, and the Red Arrows screamed over leaving skidmarks on the tiles. I made most of that up, although there were Harry Toads' pigeons. I wouldn't make them up.

It was a great day for CATSIC. So I was in a

fine and friendly frame of mind as I walked down the village that morning, greeting everyone with the smile they expect from their Vicar. Vicars are not allowed to look miserable. Vicars deprived of their favourite food aren't allowed to look miserable. Even the time Hilary left me for a few days, I was expected to look happy, because if Jesus loves you, what have you got to be miserable about? Big Jim hooted as he passed me in his Cadillac. Strange, I thought. He could have used the car's horn.

It was a fine, bright morning, just the day for chainsawing down the huge unsightly cypress hedge that blotted all the light out from number seventeen, so Alan was up there on a pair of steps, doing just that. Alan, who is lifeguard at the Huffleigh All-night Car Wash, lives at number fifteen, and he'd let his hedge get out of hand, because he never saw it in daylight, and Henry Stebbings has been grumbling about it for a long time. He has to keep his lights on all day, and his children have mildew. People see them in the choir stalls and think our boy sopranos are Martians. I wondered what Alan would do with all that stuff once the hedge was down, because it was taking up more space lying down than it did standing up. But then don't we all?

And then there was a scream, and Alan dropped the chainsaw. It fell into the mass of branches on the ground, choked and stopped. Alan slid down the ladder, bleeding heavily from a cut just above his right knee. I ran, saw that the trousers were a write-off, and that it was a bigger job than just a sticking plaster, said 'I'll get help' and ran back down the path. Mike Curly was just passing in his filthy Fiesta, but any port in a storm and all that, so I waved frantically until he stopped.

'Alan's had an accident,' I said. 'Can you get him to hospital?'

Mike thought about it for a second. 'I can't,' he said. 'I'm late already. *Ask me some other time.*' (My italics.)

And he drove off, not even waiting to wind up his window. But then the pink Eldorado came back up the High Street. I waved to Big Jim, and he stopped, and I gabbled that Alan needed help. Alan was already turning white with the shock. Jim didn't hesitate. He pulled off his tie, and bound it around Alan's leg above the cut, and while I dithered about wondering where the nearest phone was to call for an ambulance, Jim had half carried him over to his car, placed him on the white leather passenger seat, leapt into the driving seat, and was off. The whole little drama had taken three minutes at the most.

Mary, Alan's wife, came out of the back gate with a towel around her wet hair like a turban. She looked puzzled. Then she saw the chainsaw and the blood on the stepladder, and looked worried. Actually, she turned pale and nearly passed out. I'm just not very good at this descriptive stuff.

'Alan cut his leg, and Big Jim's taken him to hospital,' I said.

'I thought I heard Alan call,' she said. 'I was washing my hair.'

'You did,' I told her. 'He yelled when he cut himself. Don't worry,' I said without any justification at all, 'it looked worse than it really was. Look,' I said, 'dry your hair, I'll go and get my car, and we'll follow them to Blicester hospital.'

So we did. The Amoeba grumbled a bit about having to carry Mary as well as me. Mary was very quiet on the way, once she'd found out I didn't know any more than I'd already told her, and that all I'd done was stand and dither. Blicester Hospital isn't actually in Blicester itself, but at Evenstock, which was a little village until the hospital sat on it and squashed it. Jim's car was in the car park, and I dropped Mary off at A and E before I parked my own near it. The Cadiliac had attracted the attention of the car park attendant, and a couple of other visitors, because it's that sort of car, and pink. I glanced inside. There was a lot of blood on the white leather seat, and on the floor carpet, too.

Jim was able to direct Mary to where Alan was being attended to. I sat down next to him.

'You could get off back, now,' I said. 'I can take Mary home when she's ready.'

'You're all right, Vicar,' he said. 'They say they won't have to keep him in, and I'll take them both back.'

'The car's a bit of a mess,' I said.

'That'll clean up,' said Jim. 'And if it doesn't, I can get the seat re-covered.'

'Won't that cost a lot?' I asked.

'Don't know,' he said. 'Whatever. But Alan's all right, and that's the main thing. He'll need quite a few stitches, and he'll have a hell of a scar. He'll be able to tell people it was a great white shark when he was surfing.'

'That car means a lot to you, doesn't it?' I said.

'I had to sell a lot of shares to get it,' he said. 'But you know how it is. You see something wonderful, and you just know you have to have it, whatever it costs. I saw that car, and it was love at first sight. I think I caused a one-man market crash when I sold all those shares, but it was worth it.'

I knew how he felt. I'd felt the same when I saw Hilary.

I told him what Mike Curly had said. Maybe I shouldn't have, but now I was able to feel relieved, I was able to feel angry, too. Jim thought about it.

'Some people can't be doing with blood, and accidents, can they? What if he'd said yes, and then fainted?'

I thought what a good man Jim is, refusing to see the bad side of anybody.

'Mrs Brewer came to see me yesterday,' I said. 'She wasn't happy about you giving Myrtle the same rise you've given her. She reckons Myrtle doesn't deserve it.'

'I suppose she doesn't, if it comes to that,' said Jim. 'But she'll be pleased as anything when I give it to her. What's wrong with doing someone a favour?'

'I think Mrs Brewer felt her differentials were being eroded,' I said. 'Don't worry about it. There's no pleasing her.'

It was lunchtime before I got back to the village. I had an apple to look forward to, and when I'd finished it, I wished I had another to look forward to as well.

The story of Alan's accident caused the usual sensation that anything does in a village where nothing much happens. When I'd finished my apple, to get myself out of range of food, I went into the church to put a new light bulb over the lectern, and glue St Wayne's nose back on. I found Jason in there, where he'd just dropped in to say hello, as he put it. It was his lunchtime, too, and he was wearing his overalls, and sitting on a *Church Times* so he didn't make the pew oily. I changed the bulb, and sat down next to him, in the front pew, where you can stretch your legs. If it was an aeroplane, people would pay extra for that, but in a church, not even the chief mourners at a funeral will sit there if they can help it. Rum cove, Johnny Anglican, as the Brigadier would have said.

We sat there quietly for a minute. Jason asked how Alan was, and I said I hadn't heard any more, and then Jason said, 'I was right, though.'

'What about?' I asked.

'About the car,' he said. 'Remember when we were talking about what car Jesus would have driven? Well this morning, Jesus was definitely driving a Cadillac Eldorado. A pink one.'

    'No,' I said. 'Jim was in the driving seat. Jesus was the one doing the bleeding.'

Chapter 9

Be thou my venison

What I said about volunteering by default, by not stepping back when everyone else does, starts at a very early age. Which is why the boys had the honour of looking after the School Stick Insects for half-term. There were twelve of them, allegedly, but they were all identical, and they lived with a lot of privet in a glass tank with a lid. As pets go they were pretty unexciting. Come to think of it, they weren't even pretty, but the boys insisted that they live with us in the sitting room, not in their room, so we could all enjoy them.

The weekend went well. So did Monday. But the very next morning the lid was off the tank, and there were, as far as we could tell, no stick insects in it at all. The boys were horrified. It was like one of those pictures in children's comics that say: 'There are twelve ice creams hidden in this picture! Can you find them all?'

There seemed to be stick insects on the curtains, up the walls, on the picture frames and under the seats of chairs, inside the lampshades and pretending to be

an extra hand on the clock.
We found eleven.

I thought that was really
good, but the boys were
adamant, because the missing
one was their favourite, Sticky.
I had to get to clergy chapter,
because if you turn up late
you miss the best bit, but
the boys were not to be
deterred.

'Look,' I said, 'Eleven out of twelve is ninety-two per cent. If Beau Stebbings had looked after them, they wouldn't have had that sort of return rate.' Beau Stebbings is called Beau because his parents have so many boys they've run out of sensible names.

'But Miss Jolly *trusted* us!' said the boys. 'We said we'd look after them. Help us look!'

The boys hung on to a trouser leg each, so walking to the car was like wading through syrup, but eventually I shook them off and left them to it.

I tried to interest the clergy chapter in a discussion on the rights and wrongs of supermarkets, especially if they were going to dwarf your church, and cause dissension and schism in the rural community, and how the Vicar could be instrumental in having the plans turned down. I was feeling quite pleased with myself really, thinking I was at last emerging as a leader in the community, but they would have none of it. All they wanted to talk about was the rumour that was circulating in the deanery about the mysterious Masked Vicar who rode into a parish, righted all the wrongs, gave the PCC a good slapping if necessary, and then rode off again, his job done, with a hearty 'Hi ho, Silver!'

And the ginger nuts were soft, too.

Back in the village, what seemed to be upper-most in people's minds was weight. Mine was still not so much on my mind, as around my middle. I was convinced that there was a six-pack of rippling abdominal muscle in there somewhere, playing hard to get. But Mrs O'Chairs and Mrs Hopkins were behaving like a mini roundabout just outside the Stores, holding as animated a discussion as is possible when both of you are holding two carrier bags full of groceries.

The words every clergyman dreads are: 'The Vicar will know – let's ask him.' And before I could escape into the Stores, Mrs O'Chairs had caught me by the pot plants, and asked, 'Is it possible to keep to the Watkins Diet if you don't believe in Dr Watkins, and don't read any of his books?'

Mrs Hopkins weighed in immediately. 'It's not that I don't believe in him. I'm sure he was a very clever man. But I can have my meals, and not eat bread and potatoes and rice and spaghetti, without reading books about it.'

'But the books are the important thing,' said Mrs O'Chairs. 'They're our guide to what we can eat and what we can't and the whole *philosophy* behind it all. He's a great man, is that Dr Watkins.'

'Isn't he dead?' I asked.

'Only in the sense that he died,' said Mrs O'Chairs. 'But as long as we have the books, and as long as we keep to his way of eating, he'll always be sort of . . .'

'Still dead?' I suggested.

'But you can't do everything he says,' said Mrs Hopkins. 'Nobody can. We're all only human. You just have to do the best you can.'

'You can't pick and choose,' insisted Mrs O'Chairs, with fervour. 'It has to be all or nothing.'

'Well, I just carry on eating what I want,' said Mrs Hopkins, 'and quite a lot of that is what Dr Watkins says is all right. So I'm on the Watkins Diet, even if I don't follow everything he says to the letter.'

'If you take Dr Watkins out of the Watkins Diet,' argued Mrs O'Chairs, 'what do you have left?'

'The Diet,' I said, pleased with my own wit.

'Exactly,' agreed Mrs Hopkins. 'It's still a diet, when all's said and done.' And she eased her bulk into her car, even though she lives in the High Street only a few hundred yards from the Stores. Mrs Hopkins gave up burning calories about the same time the rest of us gave up burning Catholics. Mrs O'Chairs sighed. 'I wish I knew how to convince her,' she said. 'There must be some metaphor I could use to make it plainer.'

'I'll give it some thought,' I said. The great Diet

Revival was having unexpected consequences.
There were rumours of an extremist group of Bun
Handlers, who met in each other's houses with evangelical zeal to drink tea. At the climax of the meeting, sticky buns were passed around on plates, and
people took them, just to prove they could, without
eating them. What happened to the unfortunate
buns after these weird sessions remained a mystery.
But there was also a body of opinion that declared
with an admirable lack of zeal that All Diets Lead
To Weight Loss. Except that a lot of dieting seemed
to be going on, and not a lot of weight loss. Personally, I was suffering from the paradoxical fact that
dieting makes you more hungry.

At least the mood in the General Stores was
cheerful. I believe the right word is 'jubilant', but
this is not a village that has had much experience
of jubilant, so it was hard to be sure. We normally
rely on the papers to tell us when to celebrate.
Everyone had their own idea about why the supermarket plan had been turned down. The CATSIC
committee held that the petition had done it, while
others preferred to think that
simple commonsense had pre-
vailed. And there were some,
who had looked forward to
lucrative careers tidying the
trolleys in the car park, who
thought there was a dark
conspiracy, with deals
done and money chang-
ing hands, that had

unjustly thwarted a legitimate plan to introduce the twentieth century to the village. The twenty-first was too much to hope for, but they would have settled for a decent shop. As it turned out, rejoicing at the rejection of the plans was premature and short-lived. But more of that later. I'm trying to build up some suspense here.

The male squatters were in front of Vineyard Cottage, and at first glance it looked as if they were just working on a motorbike engine. They had grease up to their elbows, and one of them was scrubbing oil and grime off some intricate component with a toothbrush. The smile on his face suggested that it might have been his own toothbrush. He had teeth like Stonehenge, and whistling was clearly an effort.

On closer inspection, however (and the best I could do was glance out of the corner of my eye from the other side of the road), it was clear that they were ignoring a Court Order – possibly more than one. They were ignoring it blatantly, and comprehensively. We vicars know these things.

Jason came to see me that afternoon. I asked him in, took him into the kitchen and made him coffee. I could tell by his demeanour that he was agitated. He rolled up a cigarette nearly as thick as the match he lit it with. I gave him my undivided attention. He was angry, or upset, or something. I hoped he wasn't finding the prospect of marriage more trouble than it was worth, but when I asked how Melony was, a brief smile flickered across his face, and he said, 'She's great, thanks.' So I let him finish his roll-up, which took him three drags, and asked him what the trouble was.

He was indignant. 'He's only sacked me,' he said. 'Derek Morris has only given me a week's notice!'

'Why?' I asked, not because I couldn't guess, but because it seemed expected of me. I put on my all-purpose sympathetic face.

'Persistent absenteeism,' he said, as if he'd made a great effort to remember the expression. 'Whatever that means,' he added. 'Maybe he explained that bit one day when I was skiving off.'

'What will you do?' I asked.

'Well, I'm not going back on benefit,' he said. 'And I'm not going to live off Melony.' (Melony is a nurse. She only has to lean over a male patient's bed, and they feel better.) 'I can work, and I'm going to. Melony would kill me.'

He sat a moment, trying to deal with this setback. Having become a Christian, life had looked up for him generally, and I was afraid this might stretch his fragile new faith too far.

'What gets me,' he said, 'is that Morris is so soft on everyone else. Nobody pays him on time. They say, "End of the month?" and he says, "Fine", and the end of the month comes and goes, and there's people in this village that owe him from years back, literally. And just because I do one little bit of persistent absenteeism, he gives me the boot. What's today?'

'Tuesday,' I said. 'Why?'

'I've got an idea,' he said. 'See you.' And he was gone.

Things could get worse, and they
did, at dinnertime. There was the
bag, but where were the
doughnuts? I asked the boys.

'We thought they were for
us,' they said. 'There were
two of them. We thought
they were a reward.'

'What for?'

'Finding Sticky,' they said. 'He was pretending to
be a pencil. A green pencil. Aren't you pleased?'

'Ecstatic,' I said, 'but just now I'm too weak with
hunger to dance.'

'Have tea with us,' they said expansively. 'It's
spaghetti.'

'That's an S. This is a D-day,' I explained.
'Doughnuts is about all I can eat.'

'They had jam in, and everything,' they said,
which didn't help.

'What sort of diet is it,' asked Hilary, stirring a
saucepan of spaghetti with one hand, and another
of bolognaise sauce with the other, 'that means you
can eat a whole bag of doughnuts?' If she'd been
kneading bread with her toes, I wouldn't have been
surprised.

'It depends how big the bag is,' I said. 'This one
was pretty titchy, really.' I went to the fridge. There
were a couple of those triangular cheese things that
begin with a D, but that was about it.

'Why don't you just eat with us?' pleaded Hilary.
Eating should be something we all do together. It's

about the only thing
we do do together,
and now you're doing
your own thing.'

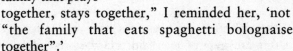

'I think the
proverb is "The
family that prays
together, stays together," I reminded her, 'not
"the family that eats spaghetti bolognaise
together".'

'So do you want some?' asked Hilary, 'There's
plenty.'

And it smelt pretty good, too. But then tempta-
tion always does seem attractive. That's how adul-
tery happens.

'You could say it's dinner with a D,' she said.

I must admit, I wavered.

'No thank you,' I said. 'I'll eat these cheesy
things.' I turned to the boys.

'And I hope you're sorry,' I said.

They looked down, sheepishly. 'Not really,' they
said, 'we did have a doughnut.' Then they looked
up brightly. 'So tomorrow will be an E-day,' they
said. 'And you know what you can eat on an
E-day?'

'Tell me,' I said.

'Ennything!' they said.

Chapter 10

Blessed asparagus

Nothing much happens in Cheeving Halfpenny. Guns are part of everyday life, but that doesn't mean that anything happens with them. It's just understood that there are farmers, and keepers, and sportsmen, and they have guns. Being what is known for the purpose as a Clerk in Holy Orders, I have a regular stream of visitors asking me to endorse their firearm certificate applications, and to verify that 'this photograph is a current true likeness' of the farmer, keeper, or sportsman who keeps a shotgun. I have no idea why being the Vicar qualifies me for this honour, but I do it, and if anybody chooses to offer me a fiver for my trouble, I accept it with thanks, and take it to the Temporary Sign, where Arthur exchanges it for beer. In any case, the photograph may well be a true likeness, but it always makes whoever it is look like a serial killer. I don't know about a 12-bore, but from the picture, I wouldn't trust any of them with a bicycle pump. I remember Charlie, who was in his eighties, who sat in his cottage in Pighill with a girlie magazine and a bottle of whisky, and a lethal weapon propped against his armchair. It was Belgian, made in 1912 (don't go thinking I'm an expert – it was written on it), had a bolt action like a rifle, and fired scale model cartridges. The barrel was too short to be legal, so Charlie had jammed a length of copper pipe over the end, painted it black, and fooled nobody. He told me that without a word of a lie, Vicar, he had once shot fourteen rats in a single afternoon without stirring from this chair. He never said whether the back door was open or not at the time.

Trying to have a day off doesn't always work. Unless I can go away somewhere, or take Hilary out for the day, somebody is bound to find me, or I'll find something that really needs doing, and slip into working the way other people slip into skiving. Maybe I should announce in the magazine that Monday is my day off, but even when people know they still ring up and say, 'I know it's your day off, Vicar, but . . .' And in any case, if the parishioners are really friends, I'm not going to tell a friend I've got no time for them just because it's a Monday.

Which is why Darkie Bloat was sitting at the kitchen table on my day off while I filled in his little form. Darkie is really called Paul, but people remembered that his father had been a black American soldier, and therefore as far as anybody in Ferret's Bottom was concerned, he's black, even though he's whiter than me and has greying red hair. Darkie has never done a day's work in his life, yet he always has money, and he has no actual convictions for anything. He even pays his road tax, which is considered an aberration in Ferret's Bottom. His son Shane, was, after all, currently serving a sentence for the Great Griping St Todger Post Office Heist. And Darkie's gun, I knew, would be used exclusively for poaching, rather than the stated vermin control. You'd have to be overrun with rats the size of bull terriers to need a 12-bore to control them. I declared I'd known Paul Bloat for eight years in the capacity of parishioner and friend, and that the photograph, looking more than usually like a mass murderer, was a current true etcetera. And then my conscience smote me, and I waved away the proffered fiver. Having Darkie think I was a gentleman seemed reward enough.

'Guess who went to see Shane in the nick?' he said, and before I could he said, 'That Jason Orrell. He thought he'd come to gloat.' Darkie shook his head in bewilderment. 'But he was real good, asked if there was anything he wanted, and slipped him two packets of snout.'

It was half-term. Mysterious noises had been coming from the boys' room all morning. At one point, they appeared briefly to ask for a bin bag. This could mean one of several things. They were going to turn it into a gas balloon, and launch some small, easily duped mammal on an aeronautical career. Or they might be using it to wrap something too ghastly for parents with only normally robust stomachs to see, or . . . We were certainly surprised when they brought it down full of rubbish and asked for another one.

Whatever they were doing stopped for lunch. They ate as if they hadn't been fed since Easter, and Hilary asked, as casually as she could, 'What have you been doing all morning?'

They said, 'Looking for something,' thanked God and Hilary, and dashed back upstairs.

'Probably the secret of turning yoghurt into gold,' said Hilary. 'Or the best way to breed rats. Or another whole new way of winding us up.'

It was mid afternoon when they appeared suddenly, with smiles the size of watermelons on their faces, carrying a Lego spaceship of more than usual size and complexity.

'Found it!' they cried.

'It's two feet long,' I commented. 'How could you lose it?'

'Not the whole thing,' they said, and pointed to a small transparent brick halfway down the port side, between the particle beam transmitters and the shield generators. 'This bit.'

'Is that what you've been turning your whole room out for?' I asked.

'Yes,' they said, surprised I should have to ask. 'We wanted to finish it, and we couldn't without that bit. And now it's finished. Isn't it great?'

We admitted it was great, and little Lego spacemen were happy with it all the rest of the day.

Jason appeared at the Vicarage door, a puzzled expression on his face.

'Darkie Bloat just waved to me from his car,' he said.

'Is that news?' I asked.

'He usually tries to run me over,' he said.

'He appreciated your going to see Shane,' I said. And somewhere among all the scars and stubble and studs, I swear Jason blushed. And then the boys cut his embarrassment short.

'Look, Jason,' they said, waving the spaceship an inch from his stubble, 'We found it!'

'Good,' he said. 'How did you lose it?'

'We're talking one little brick here,' I explained. 'The spaceship wasn't complete without it.' But the boys had gone.

'I've had a busy week,' said Jason. 'I had this idea, see? You know how I said how bad people are at paying, and how soft Derek Morris is about asking? Well, I went to his office, and looked out all the unpaid invoices. There were dozens of them. Some of them went back two years, and there were several customers had more than one. So I took them, and I've been going to see these people in the evenings. Not leaning on them,' he said hurriedly. But Jason wouldn't have to lean. He could just show up, with his studs and his mullet, and he would look as if he was leaning. And if he had Lennox the Rottweiler in tow, that lean would look quite alarming.

'Anyway,' he went on, 'one chap owed Derek a hundred and eighty quid, parts and labour. I said, give me a hundred and fifty now, and I'll give you a receipt. So he did. Another chap, no names, no packdrill, owed him three separate bills that came to near six hundred quid. I said, give me five hundred, here's your receipt, and you'll hear no more. By last night, I'd got nearly seven thousand pounds, cash and cheques, and I gave it all to Derek this

morning. His chin hit
the bench. I said,
"Can I keep my job,
then?" and he says
he'll think about it,
and tell me before
Monday. What do
you think?'

'I think
you should
be the church
treasurer,' I said.
'Or at least be a
sidesman.'

He raised an eyebrow, and it was like a ferret
pumping iron.

'Take the plate around,' I explained with a grin.

The phone rang. Jason waved a grubby thumb,
and let himself out.

I answered the phone, still smiling. It was Paul
Gruntle.

'Our Karen's on her way up to see you,' he said.
'She wants you to christen her baby.'

'Fine,' I said, the smile disappearing. 'I was going
out, but I won't, now.' ('Rats', I thought, 'I was
going to have a day off, but I won't now.')

'I hope you'll say no,' he said.

'Why might I do that?' I asked.

'She still hasn't said sorry, she doesn't say where
she's been or what she's been doing and she won't
say who the baby's father is. Although anyone can
see he wasn't one of us.' There was a nasty tone in
his voice I could almost see.

'None of that means I shouldn't baptize him,' I said.

'What about repentance and forgiveness?' he almost shouted. 'Doesn't that come into it?'

'Not always in that order,' I said. 'Maybe if you treat her normally, and show her you still love her, she'll come to see how much she hurt you, and be sorry, and say so. Maybe if you treat her like an outcast, she'll go off again and never come back.'

'You give her a good rollocking,' he said. (Well, he didn't, actually, but it was something like that.) 'That's what vicars are supposed to do.'

I said I'd have to look that one up in my book of instructions, but he'd already put the phone down.

Hilary appeared at the study door. 'There's a girl with a pushchair coming up the drive,' she said.

'Ah,' I said, bracing myself.

'Is there something you should be telling me?' she asked.

Girls with babies on the doorstep always make me feel a little uneasy. And then the doorbell rang. Some days it's all go. Hilary laughed and disappeared discreetly.

'Is it Karen or Shanti?' I asked, opening the door wide. She didn't bring the pushchair in, but lifted the baby from it, and then carried him, following me into the study.

'Shanti,' she said. 'Karen was somebody I used to be.'

'And this is Dilip,' I said, giving the baby my finger to hold. He was brown as a nut, with thick black hair above a high, distinguished forehead, less like a potato than most babies I get asked to baptize. Karen, or Shanti, was mousy-haired and fair-skinned.

'Thank you for not asking why he's called Dilip. People keep asking why he's called Dilip,' she said. 'Why do they think he's called Dilip?'

I like Karen, or Shanti. She's very attractive, but she's a farmer's daughter, and very practical, too. The sort of girl who would wear a thermal thong.

'Will you ever see big Dilip again?' I asked. She shook her head.

'He was then, and there,' she said, not sadly, more matter-of-factly, and I didn't say any more about it. To change the subject I asked, 'How's Dad taking all this?'

Dilip had no teeth, but was giving my finger a good gumming.

'He's being lovely,' she said. 'He's just giving me time to find my feet again. I had to borrow a lot of money to get back from Goa, and to settle some debts, and he's paid it all back for me.'

I managed to get my finger free, wiped it on the cat, who happened to be passing, and opened the filing cabinet, under B for Baptism. 'I have to fill in this little form,' I said. 'Now let's arrange a christening.'

Filling in the little form only took a few minutes. Finding out why Shanti wanted a Christian baptism for her baby, and where she was with God, took the inside of an hour. But by the time she left, she was assured that Dilip would be baptized in November, when Ted would have a little breathing space, and I was assured he would be brought up to love the Lord.

Shanti wasn't allowed to leave without being shown the boys' spaceship, the brick that had been missing, and the epic tale of the search.

'Well done,' she said. 'It happened to me once. With an earring.'

Chapter 11

When morning gilds the pies

Nothing much happens in Cheeving Halfpenny, so the wedding of Jason and Melony was a high spot in the year. We don't get so many weddings at St Gargoyle's since people stopped calling living together 'living in sin', and those that do get married can now do it in hotels, or underwater, or in the baskets of hot-air balloons, without benefit of clergy. So we make the most of it when it happens, hoping that those people who just went off to Bali and got married on the beach get really jealous. The flower ladies excelled themselves, and there was nowhere in the whole church you could look without seeing a chrysanthemum. The reliquaries had been polished until they sparkled, and St Nobby's cap was surrounded by blooms and greenery.

I had wondered for a time whether it was going to happen at all. Saturday morning, while I was listening to *Sounds of the Sixties*, there came a ring on the doorbell, and a man in a van asked me where Ferret's Bottom was. I restrained myself from making the obvious quip, and when he said he had a parcel for a Mr J. Orrell, I said I could save him the trip, because I was going to see Jason later at his wedding. So I signed for the big parcel. When the man had gone, and I'd picked up all the flower pots his van had knocked over, I looked at the package, and by the size of it I guessed it was Jason's suit for the wedding. So I took myself to Ferret's Bottom with the big parcel on the passenger seat.

Jason, right up until this Saturday, lived alone in a small, relatively new cottage built on the site of a former Blicester Corporation double-decker bus. It's a long story, but not unusual for Ferret's Bottom, where conventional cottages and houses only recently came to outnumber the caravans, railway carriages, sheds and yurts that people had squatted in. I parked the car, which is itself taking a risk in Ferret's Bottom, where the only sure way to assert ownership of a car is to sit in it, or the locals treat it as salvage.

A knock on Jason's door brought no answer, but Lennox barked furiously, and hurled himself at the woodwork. Repeatedly banging his head against Jason's front door has made Lennox the fine dog he is, bright-eyed and intelligent. I tried the handle, and it opened. Lennox stepped back, showing due respect for a man of the cloth. There was Jason, and at first I thought I'd interrupted his yoga practice, because there he was, in a perfect Ratasena, the Posture of the Drunk. Then I realized he must have been on the sofa all night, and he wasn't posing. I shook him by the shoulder. He opened one terrible eye, and closed it again, quickly.

'What's the time?' he asked.

'Twelve o'clock,' I said.

In a second he was sitting up, both eyes open, squinting against the light.

'Sorry, ten o'clock,' I said. 'My mistake.'

He groaned. I took my life in my hands, went into his kitchen, and put the kettle on.

'I'm not cut out for this,' he said, when he was halfway down a cup of coffee.

'What, marriage?' I asked, afraid he was going to back out, and thinking of my fee.

'No,' he said. 'Christianity. Last night . . .' He started to shake his head, winced, and changed his mind.

'Last night you had a drink?' I prompted him.

'Lots,' he said. 'In fact, I think somebody got really, really smashed, and I think it might have been me.'

'You're not the first Christian who's been drunk,' I said, 'and I think the Lord will forgive you. There, I was right,' I added. 'He has.'

'I must be the worst Christian since Osama bin Laden,' he said.

I thought about it. 'I don't know,' I said. 'What about the time you bought Jesus a pint when it was hot? And you went to see him in the nick, and took him some cigarettes. And you gave him your lunch, and he wears smart trainers, thanks to you. He won't forget any of that.'

'That wasn't *him*, though. That was just people.' Jason looked embarrassed. He didn't know I knew these things, and I bet there were lots of other things I didn't know about.

'I used to go out with a girl called Beryl,' I told him. 'When I was seventeen. I was madly in love with her. Worshipped the ground she walked her dog on, except it was a Yorkshire terrier. It was horrible,' I remembered. 'It was like a runaway moustache. Imagine a thousand-year-old Mars Bar, sort of brown and hairy, and you get the idea. Lennox would have eaten it for a snack between meals. She only took it for tiny walks because its legs were only two inches long and it was knackered by the time it got to the front gate. It didn't like me, and it barked when it saw me. It had a bark so high only bats could hear it. I went round there one day, and it was on a kitchen chair, and it barked, and every time it barked, it recoiled like a gun going off, until it fell off the chair. Laugh? I thought I couldn't stop.'

Jason sat there patiently, waiting for me to get to the point.

'Beryl said I couldn't possibly love her if I laughed at her dog, and she never spoke to me again, and married Jimmy Hebden, and I ran away and joined the Rolling Stones.'

'Really?' asked Jason, impressed.

'No,' I admitted. 'I made that last bit up. But God says if you love him, you have to love other people, and whatever you do for other people, you do for him. So you giving a tramp your new shoes was the same as giving them to Jesus.'

Jason scratched his chin thoughtfully. It sounded like a Japanese gardener raking gravel. 'I think a shave is called for,' he said.

'And I brought your suit,' I said. 'See you at half past two. If Melony's late, that's all right, but if you're late, she'll hold it against you for the next fifty years.'

But he wasn't late, and neither, as it happened, was Melony. It was a great afternoon.

Only the boys in the choir are expected to do weddings. The women consider themselves above it. So the boys had been inspected and disinfected, and threatened by Dennis that if there was any messing about, he'd see to it personally that their voices never broke. After 'Morning has broken', they sang 'Make me a channel of your peace', and ended with 'O Jesus I have promised', and from where I was, which was three feet away, Jason sounded pretty good, singing as if he meant it.

The happy couple emerged from the church, the bells rang, birds sang, voles frolicked, and the slow-worms arranged themselves into hearts and true lovers' knots.

The last wedding I had done was Jason's brother Warren, who had married Paprika Bloat. On that occasion, the Village Hall was entirely destroyed by the reception. (The last time an Orrell married a Bloat before that was in 1642, and it sparked off the English Civil War. It's true. Look it up. King and Parliament took opposing sides, the King supporting the Bloats, who had done him good service in the Bishops' War of 1639, and Parliament supporting the Orrells, who sold them pheasants.) So the New Hall, as it is known, was built with state-of-the-art smoke detectors, an automatic sprinkler system and a total ban on smoking on the premises. I mention this because what happened at Jason and Melony's reception wasn't anybody's fault, really, and certainly not Jason's. He was, if anything, the victim.

After the photographer had done his best with his camera, we all made our way to the New Hall. The photographer had struggled with something called Depth of Field, which meant that if Melony's face was in focus, the front of her dress wasn't, and vice versa. And Jason's face, shaved, and with most of his studs removed for the occasion, still looked like it had been made by a six-year-old out of plasticene, which is a challenge for any photographer. He even tried smearing the lens with Vaseline, which is supposed to make things look soft and romantic, but it just made Jason look like one of Dr Who's enemies.

The reception was a grand affair, with cheeky bunches of balloons all over the place, a buffet provided by a firm in Blicester who assumed, quite rightly, that the people of Cheeving Halfpenny have appetites like Norman peasants, and a proper bar, manned by Arthur from the pub, because the Temporary Sign wasn't expecting to do much trade that night. All the serious drinkers from Ferret's

Bottom were assembled to give Jason and Melony a proper party.

Speeches were kept to an absolute minimum so enjoyment could be at an absolute maximum. Warren was best man and he had started drinking early. In church, he had wobbled a bit, but he had stayed upright, and now he held the table in front of him with a white-knuckled grip. After he had tried to say the occasion was auspicious three times without success, he just said, 'The bar's open,' and so ended on a high note, and earned a heartfelt cheer. Somebody even took off Jason's CD of *Graham Kendrick's Greatest Hits*, and put some real music on instead, and soon everyone was having a good time. There were even a few Bloats there, on the grounds that they were the best man's in-laws, and nobody was drawing lines on the floor and challenging anyone else to step over. I had high hopes that the evening would continue to be good-humoured and free from violence and bloodshed.

As it grew dark outside, two of Jason's friends disappeared into the car park, looking furtive. I thought they were off to sabotage Jason's car in the traditional fashion, so I kept an eye on them from behind the curtain. From the boot of a car, they produced one of those huge firework banners, which they carried carefully between them, slapping each other's cigarettes out of their mouths as they came. Producing twine and a pocket knife, (these are people who have twine and pocket knives even in their best suits), they tied the banner to the railings outside the fire doors of the hall. Then they knocked on the window, and an accomplice inside drew the curtains, and opened the fire doors. There, crackling with golden sparks, was the word SNOITALUTARGNOC, in what was, for a few moments, a touching tribute to the happy couple. There was a massed 'Ooh!' of pleasure and surprise, and a burst of spontaneous applause. Then all the smoke from the fireworks blew in through the fire doors, completely obliterating those nearest.

The 'oohs' became coughs, the smoke alarms went off with high-pitched squeaks like a whole fleet of dustcarts reversing, and the sprinklers responded exactly as they were designed to do.

Nobody panicked. Not at first. Faces turned upwards to find out where the water was coming from, and then down again when they found out. *Then* they panicked.

What struck me as hilarious was that most of the women ran about shrieking trying to keep their clothes and hair dry, while the men stood there with one hand covering their beer. Nobody had a clue how to turn the system off.

I resent any suggestion that I am a coward, or one who turns tails as soon as a situation turns awkward. I really did remember just at that moment that tomorrow was Sunday and my sermon wasn't finished, and I had to go home and pull all those loose threads together with an 'And finally'.

Chapter 12

Within the veal

Never mind what the prayer books say; the big festivals in the church year are Christmas, Easter, Remembrance Sunday and, biggest of all, Harvest Festival. It isn't just that word had got around that we actually eat the harvest loaf after the morning service, and help it down with cheese and cider. It's that being in the middle of a farming area, everybody can see the harvest happening, and the church just reflects that. Never mind that the fields are harvested, ploughed and sown again before we celebrate. Never mind that we've suffered hay fever from the oil seed rape, and bites from some mysterious beast called the Harvest Mite, that is actually invisible, like the Sock Eating Goblin, but leaves you covered in huge red lumps. The church is always full. There are marrows, which nobody wants afterwards, and they only brought them to church because they didn't want them in the first place. They have been known to ferment, in which case they become objects of real alarm, because a good-sized marrow, swollen and emitting small puffs of carbon dioxide, can't even be touched, let alone moved.

There are stooks of corn, which Ted Gruntle

brings in, and they bring with them complete ecosystems of wildlife, which then scurry all over the church, squeaking, and are still there eating the candles in the Advent wreath months later.

But mainly there are people, who come to enjoy the hymns, and a sermon which reminds them of God's generosity, and appeals to them to pass it on. I once let Adrian the Reader preach at Harvest Festival, but his family, who insist on punctuating his preaching with cries of 'Alleluia', 'Amen to that, brother', and 'Tell it like it is', managed to get everyone so confused they didn't know whether he was asking them to give generously, or damning them all eternally.

After I'd celebrated the Harvest in St Gargoyle's, and the Army Bomb Disposal team had dealt with a rogue marrow that had actually started throbbing in the baptistery, threatening to awaken the Thing in the font, there was a more modest celebration at St Ickinsect's in the evening. The window sills were decorated with conkers and fluffy tendrils of old man's beard, we sang the familiar hymns which are all in keys my voice can't reach, well not in these trousers anyway, and I settled out of court with the old man who was threatening to sue whoever it was who shaved his beard off.

On my way back, I stopped for a much-needed pint at the Temporary Sign. There we all were, drinking and talking convivially, and commiserating with the football team who had lost in the Sunday league to the local prep school, who were only thirteen years old. Nigel the captain says Cheeving are the best team in the league, bar none, so when they get beaten, he always has an excuse, like their goal was only half the size of ours, they had seventeen men on the field or they were all armed with machine guns. Anything but accept that Cheeving aren't the finest footballers in all the land. And I don't laugh, because I'm the same about God. Even when the facts don't seem to bear it out, I'll still say, through gritted teeth, that God is good and he knows what he's doing. Nigel was just saying that the prep school's goalkeeper was six cubits and a span, when the bar fell suddenly silent, as a Stranger entered. This always happens in proper country pubs, but the regulars at the Sign have honed it to a fine art, as it has been a tradition since there were bears in the woods.

The stranger was a man in a suit, who bravely ran the gauntlet of dozens of narrowed eyes as he approached the bar, the squeak of his brogues the only sound breaking the watchful silence. But the girl on his arm looked familiar, although I couldn't think why. He was middle-aged, grey-haired, prosperous and self-confident, wearing more gold rings than necessary. She was young and attractive, and despite the make-up, I knew I'd seen her before. But where? The man in the suit was asking her what she wanted to drink. White wine and soda was one of those drinks Arthur has to look up the recipe for. The man in the suit had a glass of red.

And then in came Jason and Melony, looking very happy together, and a cheer went up from the whole bar. Melony turned around, and her bust swept a whole table full of empties to the floor. Somebody said, 'That will save the washing up,' because somebody always does. The hostile atmosphere would have evaporated anyway, because it's only there to add to the rustic charm, but the conversation buzzed again, and Arthur brightened perceptibly. Jason on honeymoon had represented a considerable blow to his profit margins.

'Did you have a good time?' I asked, trying not to smirk.

'I think so,' said Jason. 'I don't remember much of it.'

'Did you have a good time?' I asked Melony.

'I was with him,' she said.

I took that to be a yes, and bought them a drink.

'Whose is the Jag?' asked Jason.

The man in the suit turned and looked at him over his shoulder. 'Is it in your way?' he asked.

'Just admiring it,' said Jason. 'I've always wanted a Jag.'

The man looked Jason up and down with obvious disapproval.

'Well, if you cut your hair, and took out all the ironmongery, and maybe washed, and I gave you a job stacking shelves in one of my shops,' he said, 'you might work your way up, like I did, until you own the whole chain. Then you can have as many Jaguars as you want.'

Jason's Christianity had taken hold to the extent that he didn't immediately punch him on the nose, or even look as if he wanted to. He turned away, and took Melony to a table.

It clicked. I suddenly recognized the girl as Tina, the checkout girl from Saneways.

'Hello, Tina,' I said, showing off that for once I'd remembered someone's name. She looked at me, obviously not knowing me from Adam, and then she saw my collar. Adam wasn't much of a one for collars.

'It's the Vicar with the nits, isn't it?' she said, in a voice so quiet that a few people the other side of Pighill might not have heard her. Her companion looked at me.

'Do you know my . . . niece?' he asked.

'Only professionally,' I said, excused myself, and went to sit with the newlyweds. We were joined a moment later by Big Jim.

'Do you know who that is?' he asked. We all shook our heads.

'You don't read the business section in the papers, do you?'

I said I didn't, and Jason asked what a business section was.

'That,' said Jim, 'is Sir Samuel Saneway.' He paused while we all said 'No', 'Strike a light', 'Well, stap me vitals', and 'Who?'

'And the girlie with him,' went on Jim, 'is *not* Lady Helen Saneway. I wonder what he's doing here.'

'Her name's Tina, she works on the checkout at Huffleigh, and she's his niece,' I said.

'And I'm the ghost of Hamlet's father,' said Jim. 'He lives in London.' Melony looked really impressed. She thinks living in London and being important are the same thing.

'He owns property just up the road,' I reminded them. 'He's probably come to see what it's good for, now he can't have his shop.'

'He could grow potatoes,' Jim chuckled.

'Not in that field,' said Jason. 'Maize, maybe, or oil seed rape. Not potatoes.'

Within the veal

'What a country boy you are,' marvelled Jim.

'Other people have told me the same thing,' said Jason.

He got up, and went into the pub kitchen, through the terrible double doors where nothing comes out alive. Which is just as well, if you've ordered chicken in a basket. It's like Dante's inferno in there, and a grim warning to us all not to covet our neighbour's ox. Jason greeted Arthur's wife cheerfully, helped himself to two large potatoes from the paper sack that stood in the kitchen, and went out the back way into the car park. He inserted a potato into each of the exhaust pipes of the Jaguar, gave them a kick to make sure they were in firmly, and came back into the pub through the front door, where he joined us at the table with a very pleased expression on his face.

'What have you been up to?' I asked, because I didn't know then.

'Up to?' he said, as though the very thought of mischief had never entered his head.

I looked across the room, to where Tina was standing by herself at the bar. I gave her a friendly wink, and she looked away, confused. Sir Samuel was in a corner, deep in conversation with David Mortimer, the solicitor, and Andy Lefevre, the builder. I wished I was a fly on the wall to hear what they were discussing, but then if I had been, I wouldn't have understood it anyway. And Arthur would have tried to kill me.

Sir Samuel shook hands with David, and pausing only to collect Tina from the bar, he left the pub.

Jason went to the window to watch. So did I. Sir Samuel ushered Tina into the car with impressive gallantry, climbed into the driving seat, and turned the key. Nothing happened. So he tried again. The third time, he kept the key turned, until there was an explosion like Krakatoa, and a potato shot from the exhaust, narrowly missing Winnie's cat, which leapt three feet vertically, landed running, and shot down the road at forty-five miles an hour.

Sir Samuel eased himself, shaking visibly, from the car. He went round the back, where he saw nothing untoward. Gingerly, he got back in, tried again, and the car started. He drove off into the night, overtaking Winnie's cat somewhere near Griping St Todger.

'Did you see that?' gloated Jason. 'Actual flames! There were actual flames!'

Chapter 13

We love the plaice, O God

Nobody who heard about it would ever forget the day the Brigadier went to see Uncle John. It was a still, misty Friday in late October, and as I took the rubbish down the drive on the off-chance that the dustmen might be in the mood to take it away, I saw that dark deeds had been afoot. Nobody saw it arrive, except the squatters, and they wouldn't have said, but there was another yellow notice stuck on the telegraph pole, inviting anyone who could be bothered to view the revised plans at the council offices. I checked to make sure it wasn't the old one still there, but the dates were different. Another trip to Huffleigh was called for, so I checked my diary, phoned Mrs Arkwright to say I would lay hands on her as soon as I got back, and set off, eager to see what was in the mind of Sir Samuel Saneway, if he had one.

Mr Surly in his cap was still there, but behind the counter this time in the Planning Department was a spotty youth. I'm sorry if you think I'm writing two-dimensional stereotypes, but here was a lad of about fifteen summers, with hair sticking up vertically (an effect produced, apparently, by applying styling gel, and then sticking two fingers in the light socket. Don't try this at home, kids!), and more spots than *101 Dalmatians*. I showed him the reference number, and off he scampered like a puppy after a stick, and came back with the familiar buff folder and stack of drawings.

The revised plan showed the supermarket as before, or maybe a tiny bit smaller. Something had been done to the roof line, to lower it by a token amount. Next to it, and sharing its car park, was a building the size of the Village Hall, labelled 'Social Club'. Next to that was another building. I could hardly believe my eyes. It was labelled 'Community Centre/Church'. I drove back to the village in a terrible mood. Pheasants, rabbits and pedestrians leapt for the hedges as the tiny Fiat took the centre of the narrow lanes, brambles brushing both wing mirrors as I made a couple of unwise short cuts home.

It was later, while I was struggling with my sermon for Sunday, that I heard the news about the Brigadier. On that still Friday afternoon, a cockerel in the garden crowed. It stirred the dust in the archives of the Brigadier's half-forgotten folklore. Where was it? Ethiopia, or Kenya? Ethiopia, where the cockerel that crowed in the afternoon was a sign of such misfortune to come that only its death could stave off disaster.

Percy had long since dismantled his father's guns, which had been relegated to wall decorations. They ranged from a pistol, itself larger than a Colt Peacemaker, to vast artillery pieces that could blow a hole in an elephant big enough to

shout into. But the
Brigadier, often
alone in the house,
had done his
reconnaissance,
made mental
notes, and
spurred on
by the cockerel,
which repeated

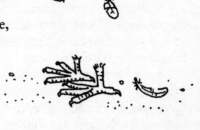

its crime at short intervals, collected from drawers
and low cupboards and the dust under Percy's bed
the pieces of an awesome weapon that looked as if
it could sink the VICTORY. Armed with this, slipping
into its breech a huge cartridge the size of a can of
beans, and with another in his cardigan pocket, the
Brigadier stepped into his garden where the fowl
was committing the offence.

The first shot raised the topsoil from a square
yard of the garden, sent the birds flying vertically
for a couple of furlongs in every direction and the
Brigadier spinning like a top, and brought the neighbours running with genuine concern. The Brigadier
reloaded swiftly.

The second shot blew an innocent chicken entirely away. Nothing was left of the hapless bird bigger
than a toenail. But this time the recoil caught the
Brigadier off-balance, and he fell backwards, striking his head on the chickens' feed-bowl.

Percy and the neighbours found him lying there,
the smoking gun clenched vertically in his grip, and
wearing the feed-bowl like a helmet. By the time the

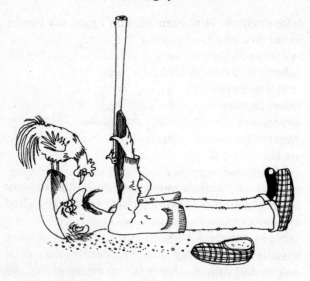

police had been, and investigated what there was to investigate, and Henry Dolt had been informed, Percy was collected enough to ask me whether the family vault in the church could be opened for his father's funeral.

Back in the village, it was getting late. I still had Mrs Arkwright on my conscience, and I was in no mood for Veggie Vera, especially as it was only Friday, and Vera is only usually a nuisance on Saturdays. But there she was, with her 'Meat Is Murder' banner, handing out little tracts. Vera lives with so many cats that all her clothes have a sort of hairy quality, and she belongs to an extreme sect of fundamentalist vegetarians that even other vegetarians find embarrassing. Her creed, which consists mainly of everybody else being wrong, is based on entirely false doctrine. But because I didn't have my hands in my pockets, and made the mistake of making eye contact, Vera thrust a small leaflet at me. It was called *The Truth about Scratchings*.

'It's quite horrible, Vicar,' she trilled. 'It's all in there, chapter and verse. Did you know that pork scratchings are made with a live pig and a cheese-grater? And when it heals up they do it all over again?'

I confessed that this fact, if it was a fact, had escaped me, and promised her I would stick to crisps in future, a promise I would have no trouble keeping.

It's bad enough with people at our own church being on the Strict Biblical Diet, which means if it isn't in the Bible, you don't eat it. No pasta, no rice, no potatoes, but you are allowed bread, whether you fetch it yourself or ravens bring it for you. You can have roast lamb, but no pork; cod but not skate, honey but no sugar, and all the burnt offerings you like. The District Council are getting worried about the drains in the village, such as they are, which date from the fifties and weren't designed to cope with all those figs. People on this diet believe it to be inspired directly by God, and claim that if the Lord had meant us to eat Mars Bars it would be there in the scriptures.

'You ought to be outside Saneways in Huffleigh,' I suggested to Vera. 'More people there to listen to your message.'

'I wasn't called to them,' she said. 'Only to my own people.'

'Which is our good fortune,' I said tactfully, folding the little leaflet into my pocket as I left her.

Friday evening found Jason in the Temporary Sign, drinking the sort of lager Jesus would have drunk. It also saw me there, enjoying a pint of real beer. Don't get the impression I spend every waking hour in the pub, but if a pastor ought to be where his people are, I rest my case. And in any case, a hurriedly convened meeting of the CATSIC committee was taking place. I would like to say that the place was packed to the walls with people, the whole village having turned out to express its feelings about the new proposal. Arthur would have liked to say it, too, but in fact only the usual suspects were present, and Arthur himself was eager to take part.

'Did you notice the new sign?' he asked.

I said I hadn't, but dutifully went outside to admire it. There, sure enough, was a picture of a large brown stag on a background of green forest trees. And written underneath, for the benefit of those who could read, it said The Stag.

'Two chaps from the brewery came this morning and put it up,' said Arthur. 'Apparently this pub is called The Stag.'

'I've been here eight years,' I said, 'and it's always been the Temporary Sign.'

'When there was another pub,' said Arthur, 'I suppose it was important. But when the other pub closed, this one was just The Pub.' If there had ever been another pub in the village, it was news to me.

'What was the other one called?' I asked.

'Queen Jane's Snickers,' said a voice from under a flat cap in a chair in the corner. It was Toby Chunt, retired wattle-dauber, who could only daub half-way up the wattle on account of being so short.

'Rubbish,' said another voice under another cap, which was Harry Toads, the pigeon fancier. 'It were Queen Anne's Bounty.'

'Same thing,' grunted Toby. 'I knew it were a queen and a bar of chocolate.' They would have been playing dominoes, except Lennox had eaten the double-blank in mistake for a charcoal dog biscuit, and the shop doesn't sell double-blanks separately, and Arthur is too tight to buy a whole new set.

'So this is The Stag,' I mused. 'That's going to take some getting used to. But I thought you were all in favour of the supermarket,' I said. 'Increased trade and all that.'

'If it was just a supermarket, yes,' he said.

Mrs General looked puzzled.

'People coming to the village with money to spend, I'd be happy to help. But a Social Club?' He sucked his teeth, and shook his head slowly.

'They've got one in Huffleigh,' said Mrs Goddard. Ladies of traditional build shouldn't sit on bar stools, but she was. 'It's lovely. There's a bar and they do food and there's two snooker tables and pool and darts and they have quiz nights and bingo and karaoke . . .' she trailed off, out of breath, and because Arthur was looking daggers, swords and those spiky balls on a stick at her.

'That's why I'm against it,' he said. 'A country pub

can't compete with that. It wouldn't be a country pub any more. And can you see Toby Chunt doing karaoke?'

I could see Toby Chunt, just, behind his beer. But even if I closed my eyes and strained, I could only see that Arthur was right.

'Trouble is,' said Mrs General, 'There's already people saying they want a Social Club, and Saneways will give us one, like the sightscreen for the cricket club, and it's us spoiling it, trying to put a – what's those things that go in the works?'

'Outing?' suggested Mrs Goddard.

'Tea urn?' from John Norman.

'Spanner,' said Mrs General. 'We're suddenly the spoilsports.'

'What bothers me,' I said, 'is this church. Why a church? St Gargoyle's has been here since the Normans' – 'It was here before us,' said John – 'and it's good for a few years yet. Who's going to go to this new church? Will it have a Vicar? Will it be interdenominational?'

The people who knew what interdenominational meant sat there waiting for the people who didn't know to ask, so they could show off. Nobody asked.

Mrs O'Chairs spoke up. 'Young people with children will find it much easier to get their shopping at the new supermarket, and there will be jobs, too. Checkouts in the day, filling shelves in the evenings, and the Community Centre will be great for the old people to sit and meet . . .' Mrs General gave a squawk like a chicken that stopped her dead.

'Whose side are you on?' she asked. 'This is CATSIC – the Campaign *Against* the Supermarket in Cheeving!'

'She's right, though,' I said. 'That's what we're up against. And if it's really what people want, should we be up against it? There's still only seven of us.'

Arthur sighed, and disappeared to spit on glasses or whatever it is publicans do when they're not serving customers. We would have carried on what looked increasingly like a fruitless discussion, but the meeting seemed to have broken up of its own accord.

'That Sir Samuel Saneway was in here again yesterday,' said Jason, putting heavy emphasis on the title. 'Talking to that lawyer chap. Mortimer.'

'Not a man who has the best interests of the village at heart,' I remarked, although it was becoming more doubtful as to what the best interests of the village really were.

'He was saying it was too soon,' went on Jason.

'Too soon for what?'

'I didn't hear. I wasn't actually earwigging. I just overheard Sir Samuel say it had gone in too soon, and should have waited till the middle of next month.'

I was wondering what that might mean, if anything, when we were interrupted. Mike Curly, he of the unwashed Fiesta, came into the pub, and immediately offered to buy Jason a drink. Jason accepted, and soon had a fresh pint in front of him.

'This man's a star,' said Mike to me. 'Did me a favour. Saved me a bit of money.'

'It seems you've made a friend,' I said. Then in came a stout man I didn't know, with a suit and a prosperous air, who ordered a gin and tonic. Arthur looked a bit puzzled, because he doesn't get asked for them very often. The stout man handed over a note, and said, 'Put one in for my friend here,' nodding towards Jason.

'Another satisfied customer,' said Jason, sotto voce. 'I took four hundred quid off Mike, but saved him fifty. Derek wouldn't have got anything off him, ever. He's so tight you'd have to run him under the hot tap to loosen him.'

'Even if Derek doesn't take you back,' I said, 'it looks like you've got friends. Maybe you could go into business on your own account!'

Jason's face probably lit up, but with all the rings, studs and stubble, it was hard to tell. 'Maybe I could,' he said.

Chapter 14

Lord, for the beers

Angry? I was furious! I was in the vestry, changing the cheese in the mousetraps, and in the cupboard where the coffee things are kept for after the service, I found a huge, half-full jar of coffee. Not the Fairtrade coffee we use on a regular basis, but Saneways own-brand granules. So I gave Shirley a ring, because she is supposed to be in charge, and she confessed. She has been filling the coffee jar out of the big one from Saneways, because it's so much cheaper, and she says nobody can tell the difference. The church has only ever bought one jar of Fairtrade coffee, and recycles the jar.

'You'd be mad to pay more,' she said. 'Saneways say so.'

'What about ethics?' I asked.

'What about it?' she countered. 'This is Dorset.'

'But we're a church. We ought to be setting an example, and helping people in developing countries. That's what Fairtrade is about. And I *can* tell the difference. No wonder I find it hard to stay awake when I'm doing the service at St Ickinsect's, if all I've had here is a cup of own brand.'

'We're also a church,' she interrupted, 'that has trouble finding its share, and I was only trying to help.'

I made her promise no more cheating, and definitely no more Saneways own brand. Back at the Vicarage, I had a good sniff of the jar of coffee. Completely different. Then I had a cup of it, because a sniff didn't really do anything for me. Then I decided that my other parish wasn't getting a fair crack of my whip, and steered the Amoeba over to Pighill. There was a Sold sign outside The Cottage (every house in Pighill is called The Cottage), which hadn't been there the last time I'd visited.

The largest house in Pighill was once the Rectory, and now that the Rector is me, Mrs Baring lives there. Mrs Baring either has the world's hairiest armpits, or two very small dogs. She is an incomer, of course. Her late husband made a fortune from betting shops, which she strenuously denies; if anybody asks, she says he was 'in books'. Over the door of the house is a coat of arms, partly so she can say she is one of the armorial Barings, but also because nobody else in the village has one, or has ever wanted one. The shield shows a freshly kicked peasant, with the motto *Super Corpus Meum*, or Over My Dead Body. The Barings have spent six hundred years opposing everything, from the Reformation, the Bible in English, the abolition of slavery, women's suffrage, the Alternative Service Book, the compact *Times* and the blue Smartie. Mrs Baring sized me up the first time she saw me, decided I was of the Coffee Mug Class rather than the Best China Cup Class, and so there we sat, me with a mug of steaming instant, and she with her dinky cup.

I told her what
people had said,
about how some
people would
welcome a super-
market in the vil-
lage. Her eyebrows
actually shot clear
of her head, and
hovered a moment
in mid air, like
hairy cater-
pillars on a
trampoline.

'Out of the question,' she announced firmly. 'This village has never had a shop, and certainly doesn't need a supermarket.' She pronounced 'supermarket' to rhyme with 'brothel'.

'A lot of the older people would appreciate not having to walk half a mile to the bus stop to catch a bus to Huffleigh,' I said. 'Even a little shop would make life easier for them.'

'But it wouldn't be our little village any more,' said Mrs Baring.

'It might be better,' I said.

'Nothing changes for the better,' she insisted. 'You know things are much better left alone.'

We changed the subject. The people who have moved to the village don't want it to change from the way they first saw it, and the people who have lived there all their lives, and watched its subtle changes over the years, find it puzzling that their shed or pigeon loft is seen as an eyesore, or the noise of farm animals and machinery is described as disturbing the peace. And it isn't the older church-goers who object to the Bible being read in church in a language they can understand, but Mrs Baring, whose ancestors saw the King James Version as absolutely the last time they would have the scriptures messed about with. A church that used a modern form of worship that young people might want to come to wouldn't be Our Little Church any more. Mrs Baring once told me that as long as the church was there to bury her, she wasn't worried about what happened afterwards.

'I notice The Cottage has been sold,' I remarked.

'Yes,' she said with satisfaction. 'We finally persuaded them that this isn't the village for them. They never fitted in.'

'They came to church,' I reminded her.

'And then complained that it wasn't to their liking,' she sniffed. 'They were,' and she looked about as if someone might have been eavesdropping from behind the arras, '*Evangelicals*'.

'You mean . . .'

'They wanted the New International Version.'

I was clearly expected to recoil in horror, but I didn't. I told Mrs Baring about the Brigadier's death, so she could stop the rumour spreading that he had shot himself. And then I finished my coffee and excused myself, because the accumulated effect of all that coffee was taking its toll on my attention span, if you get my meaning, and I had to get back to Cheeving, and do dark deeds in a dingy recess of the parish church.

In the front right-hand corner of St Gargoyle's is a little chapel that everybody thinks is the Lady Chapel, but it isn't. The motif of linked sausages carved in the stonework ought to be a clue. This chapel is dedicated to St Botulus of Salamis, the patron saint of sufferers from food-poisoning, and most people don't realize that the stubby candle usually burning on the window ledge is placed there by Mrs General, just in case. It's the only time she comes into church on any regular basis. In the floor of the chapel, among the worn flagstones, some still bearing fragmentary inscriptions, is one with an iron ring set into it, and this is the entrance to the Hollywoods' crypt, where generations of the Brigadier's ancestors have been laid to rest. I had never been in there, or even been particularly curious to do so, but now it had to be done. If there was a space in there for the Brigadier, he needed it.

I asked Jason to come along because it was lunchtime, and I found him standing around not doing anything, still wondering if he would have a job after the weekend. I thought a bit of brute force would probably be needed, and he thought to bring a torch, too. But I decided that an electric one would be better, even if, as Jason said, his torch, made of tarred felt wrapped around a three-foot stick, would have been more dramatic. As it turned out, dramatic would have been the wrong word altogether. Catastrophic would have been better.

'Get a hold of that ring,' I said, 'and let's have that stone up.'

Jason managed to get both hands around it, and

gave it a good heave, but nothing happened, except the veins on his forehead became more pronounced. Then he had an idea. He unbuckled his belt, slipped it out of the loops in his jeans, and passed it through the iron ring. He held one end himself, gave the other to me, and we both pulled. There was a noise like a large flagstone lifting from its resting place, as the large flagstone gradually became vertical. Jason straightened himself up with a satisfied look on his face, and his jeans fell down. It was one of those moments that *Simpsons* underpants are made for.

By the time Bart was decently inside Jason's trousers again, and his belt was back on, I was shining the torch down the hole.

'There's no need to apologize,' I said. 'God can see your underpants anytime he wants to.'

'That's a thought,' he said, doing up his buckle. 'If God knows everything, does that mean he *has* to know everything? I mean, there's stuff I'd rather not know, even if I could.'

We were looking down the square black hole in the chapel floor. All I could see in the beam of the torch was the floor, about seven feet below.

'Steps would have been nice,' said Jason, peering into the darkness. He was right. The only way to get down there was to jump. The Brigadier's funeral, which would involve manoeuvring a coffin down there, would be quite complicated, apparently, and if we didn't watch it, downright comical. Henry Dolt is quite capable of making an ordinary burial into a news story, and this one had any number of ways of going pear-shaped.

'I'll hold the torch for you,' offered Jason.

'Or I could hold it for you,' I countered.

Neither of us was in a hurry to go into a dark crypt full of coffins. I'd read *Moonfleet*, and Jason had seen the film, in the days when he was able to spend whole afternoons watching Channel 4. But people in villages still expect the church to represent authority, and look to their Vicar for leadership, which was why I was in the mess I was, so eventually I plucked up all my courage, and just *told* Jason to get down the hole. He sat himself on the edge, took his weight on his hands, and let himself go. There was a bit of unseemly cursing, followed by some seemly repentance, and then he reached up for the torch. A moment later there was a loud exclamation, and his voice, echoing strangely, suggested that I ought to see for myself. I went to the vestry, found the stepladder I use to change the light bulb in the statue of St Barry, and lowered it into the crypt.

'How come you have a stepladder?' asked Jason.

'It was Hilary's before I married her,' I explained.

'Why couldn't I use it, then?'

'Because I was the one who thought of it,' I said.

The next minute, I shared Jason's exclamation. The beam of the torch, together with the little light from the trapdoor, gave us quite a shock. The crypt was full, not of coffins, but barrels.

It *was* just like *Moonfleet*. The barrels were each about a foot and a half high, and I could see about twenty. Remember what I said about the village

living off smuggling in the old days? Obviously it was still going on. A gang of smugglers was storing its smuggle in the church, and not even offering me a percentage. And then Jason, his lips moving with the effort, read what it said on one of the barrels.

'Gunpowder.'

First I wondered who would want to put a load of gunpowder in the crypt of St Gargoyle's, and then I thought, anybody who saw the church as an obstacle to their planning application and was also quite mad.

'It could have been worse,' said Jason.

I asked him how.

'I could have had a fag on,' he said.

'We have to get out of here,' I said, and we took ourselves up the steps, pulled them out of the hole, and let the stone back down into its place.

146

Jason said, 'They didn't get it down there through the trapdoor, did they? There must be a way in from the outside.'

Now I know it's only eight years, but it feels like I've been Vicar of St Gargoyle's since the earth was hot, and I knew nothing about another entrance to the crypt. Jason and I went outside, and round to the south-east corner, where there are a couple of those old tombs like stone tables, and one with iron railings around it. It's full of long grass and sycamore seedlings because you can't get a strimmer in there, so it's in the local guidebook as the World's Smallest Park, and people come to look at it. Then Jason pointed to a flat stone slab on a low plinth, about a foot off the ground, nearly up against the church wall. Some of the long grass around about was trapped under it. Someone had moved the slab recently. I beckoned Jason away, and we went back round the church to the kissing-gate that leads out into the field that all the fuss was about. We leaned on the wall, trying to look casual.

'What we do,' I said, 'is we pretend we've seen nothing. This must have been done under cover of darkness, so we keep a watch at night, and when someone comes to set it off, we'll see who it is.'

'And kick 'em in the nuts,' added Jason.

'No!' I said. 'What would Jesus do?'

'Oh. Right. Sorry.' He thought about it a long time. Then he said, 'I give up. What would Jesus do?'

'I haven't a clue,' I admitted. 'But definitely not

kicking them in the nuts. He'd have loved them and forgiven them, but I bet he'd have talked them out of blowing the church up first.'

'But Vicar,' Jason said, 'we don't know when they might come back. We might have to wait every night for a month or more.'

'I don't think so,' I said. 'What's today?'

'Thursday,' he said.

'And?'

'Dustbin day.'

'The date, Jason!'

'The third. November the third.'

'Exactly. And Saturday is November the fifth. They can blow it up then and everyone will think it's an accident.'

'You mean that in among all the rockets and Roman candles,' Jason said, 'everyone will think the church blowing up is just a fireworks accident? I don't think so, Vicar! They aren't going to look at a smoking ruin and say "I bet that one cost a couple of quid".'

'I still have a hunch,' I said.

'You should keep your shoulders back,' he said.

'Remember when you overheard David Mortimer and Sir Samuel Saneway in the pub?' I said. 'Sir Samuel said the new application had gone in *too early*. This is it. The new plan wasn't supposed to go in until the church wasn't there any more, so the new church was going to be instead, not as well.'

'Is that what you call a fiendishly cunning plan,' Jason wondered out loud, 'or the stupidest thing I ever heard?'

But we went back into the church, lowered the flagstone carefully back in place, and made our way back through the damp churchyard to the Vicarage, pleased to have uncovered the dastardly plot, and determined that Saneways weren't going to get away with it.

Chapter 15

Beef or the throne

The sound of an ambulance siren in Cheeving Half-penny always causes anxiety. I find myself praying, illogically, that it isn't for anyone I know. When I heard it stop, I went down the drive, and saw it was outside Vineyard Cottage. I thought perhaps one of the squatters might have come to some harm, but it was a stranger I watched being stretchered into the ambulance. I asked Alan, who was standing there with his mobile phone in his hand, and he told me it was Jamie Stern, and he'd been beaten up by the people in the cottage. I hadn't seen Jamie since he was about twelve, when he went away to one of those schools that make a man of you.

'Have you called the police?' I asked.

Alan shook his head. 'He said not to. Just before he passed out.'

'I'll get off to the hospital and see him this afternoon,' I said.

I packed some muesli bars and a flask of hot coffee. A visit to the hospital at Evenstock is not to be undertaken lightly, especially when the November mists shroud its corridors, and the short days give way to darkness that can leave you stranded in the featureless wastes between the stroke unit and the

GUM clinic, where the notices are so discreet you can't see them at the best of times. After several days of trekking through the trackless wastes, the muesli bars gone, and I was thinking of eating my dog collar, I finally found Saddam Ward, where Jamie Stern lay in bed. Even if I'd seen him since he grew up, I wouldn't have recognized him, because his face looked like a Picasso. But he managed a smile.

'I don't need the last rites yet, Padre,' he said. He started to ask me how I was, and reminisce about when I was the New Vicar, but when he said he remembered me as slimmer then than I am now, I got down to brass tacks.

'How are you feeling?' I asked.

'I feel as if I've been beaten up by four Hell's Angels and their girlfriends,' he admitted.

'Anything broken?'

He shook his head, and winced with pain. 'Nothing broken,' he said, 'but I'm going to miss all the fun.'

'What fun?' I asked.

'Dad's home,' said Jamie. 'He's back from Belize, and he wants his house back. I was their last warning.'

'Is that why they beat you up? Because you're his son?'

'And because I told them they were for the high jump because Dad was in no mood for any more crap from them, and he does a pretty good impression of a ton of bricks.'

'Have the police been told?' I asked.

He nodded. 'Dad wouldn't do anything actually outside the law,' he said. 'Some of his best friends are coppers. But he'll do it his own way, in his own time.'

Meanwhile, we had our own agenda to pursue. Don't think for a moment we did nothing on the few nights before the fifth of November. They were dark and moonless, just the thing for dirty deeds, and in case my theory was wrong, every evening we rigged tripwires across the churchyard, attached at one end to the church drainpipes, and at the other to bunches of empty cans balanced on the altar-tombs, so nobody could approach the entrance to the crypt without making a lot of noise. Jason seemed to have an inexhaustible supply of empty cans. I slept badly, with one ear cocked in case Guy came. (Jason and I had given our conspirator the name Guy, after his famous predecessor, Guy Conspirator.) I had said nothing to Hilary, because I knew she would say 'Go to the police' over and over again until I did.

The fifth was a dry night, still and clear.

'Where actually is heaven?' asked Jason, peering up at the sky, which was more than usually spectacular. People who come from cities look at our night sky and say 'Wow!' because we have so few streetlights. There was a sliver of a new moon, like God winking.

'I don't know if heaven really is a place,' I whispered. 'It used to suit people to think of heaven being up there, and hell being down there, because it had a sort of neatness about it. I think heaven could be a sort of other dimension.'

'That makes as much sense as anything,' said Jason. 'If I know Melony is around, I can be happy anywhere.'

Despite what happened last year, the boys had been invited to a bonfire party at the Stebbings's. The cat was safely locked indoors, and when Jason had arrived with Lennox on a short lead, I told Hilary I was just going out. I could probably keep a mistress, because if I tell Hilary I'm just going out, she never asks where, or where I've been when I come back. So people really can rely on my being the soul of discretion, right up to the point where I decide to write a book. Jason and I looked around the darkness, and found ourselves suitable positions to watch from. Jason sat comfortably with his back against a tombstone, still marvelling at the beauties of creation, with Lennox dozing beside him. I positioned myself the other side of the entrance slab, crouched rather less comfortably behind the tomb of Minifred Hyssop, late of this parish.

The fireworks started soon after dark. Some people had parties in their gardens, with modest displays. In the distance, towards Griping St Todger, there was a bigger display, with those big rockets that go off like chrysanthemums, and the sort of bangs that could cover up a murder. Lennox hardly stirred. A dog that has lived with Jason, and taken part in his nocturnal activities when he was still steeped in sin, wasn't going to be bothered by a few fireworks. I began to wonder if anyone would hear a medieval church explode and say 'We must have one of those next year,' but my theory was that the destruction of St Gargoyle's on Guy Fawkes' Night might just be passed off as an accident by somebody mad enough, or desperate enough, to somebody stupid enough, and paid well enough.

We were quite prepared to wait all night, but at about eight o'clock, I heard the latch of the lych-gate click, and so did Jason. Lennox lifted an ear. Two men came up the path, nearly as far as the porch, then moved more stealthily along the wall of the church to the tomb slab. Then, before the other one could silence him with a sharp 'Shhh!' one of them began to whistle nervously through his teeth. It was the first line of 'What a friend we have in Jesus'. I recognized that whistle. They stood a moment, making sure there was nobody around, and didn't see us. With an obvious effort, but still trying to be quiet, they moved the stone back. The grating noise it made sounded loud in the churchyard. But it was quickly done, revealing a rectangle of deeper darkness, the entrance to the Hollywoods' crypt. As soon as they straightened themselves up, Jason rose to his feet, and said, loudly, 'Go, Lennox!'

Both men turned with an obvious start, and the lucky one caught Lennox, flying as if he'd been thrown, and fell over backwards into the hole. The other had Jason to face. Do you remember all those Robin Hood movies where the Sherriff's men wore chain-mail balaclavas, but they still got punched on the chin, and Robin Hood never seemed to hurt his hand? Rubbish, weren't they? But this luckless miscreant hit Jason. Then he yelled, clutching his fist in his other hand, because punching Jason is like hitting a bag of nails.

The first thug was climbing out of the hole like a character in a Stanley Spencer painting, with Lennox hot on his heels, or more precisely, the seat of his trousers. I found a bit of him relatively free of dog and sat on it, and Jason collared the other one, tripping him up neatly. He asked Lennox to be a good boy and stop chewing the one I was sitting on. Lennox let go, and subsided into deep bass growling.

Jason seized his man by the cheek, and pulled.

'Now let's see who you are under this rubber mask,' he said.

'I'm not wearing a cowing mask,' shouted the villain, 'that's my cowing face!'

'This is the bit where you tell us what you were up to, and say, "and we'd have gotten away with it, too, if it wasn't for those pesky kids".'

The answer was only two words. One of them was 'off'.

'Now,' I said, 'I'm ready to hear your confessions.'

Neither said anything.

'Come on,' I encouraged them. 'We're all friends, aren't we? And you know I'm a proper Vicar,' I said. 'I've got the collar and everything.'

They weren't convinced, I could tell.

'How about,' I suggested, 'we call the police, and we stick you down there, and my friend here can have a smoke while we're waiting.'

Even in the near darkness, we could see their eyes widen in fright.

'OK,' I said. 'Tell us all about it, and we won't call the police.'

'I don't know who he was, and that's the truth, but he's paying us a grand apiece and we was to make sure nobody was about so nobody got hurt.'

'And everyone's supposed to think it was a fireworks accident?' I prompted.

The other one nodded.

'Call the police,' I said to Jason. His mobile phone glowed in the dark like a . . . well, like a mobile phone, really.

'You said you wouldn't!' cried the prostrate felon.

'I lied,' I admitted.

The police were with us in about twenty minutes, and as soon as they saw what was in the crypt, the army was with us in another twenty, once they were persuaded it wasn't just another rogue marrow. As they were going into the church, they changed their green camouflage smocks for a coat of brown varnish. I asked very nicely if they could get all the barrels out as soon as possible, because I had a funeral in a couple of days. I don't think they heard me.

So we had the Sunday service at St Ickinsect's. St Gargoyle's was cordoned off with blue and white ribbon, and two policemen in yellow jackets stood impassively, not letting anybody in, not even to do the flowers. We thought about the Village Hall, but it was still a bit damp. Actually, it was very damp. The mousetraps were catching fish, and the children had to wear flippers for playschool. So a few phone calls, and the whole congregation went off to the other parish in the benefice. When they saw car after car arriving on the village green, the people of Pighill first thought it was a point-to-point, which always draws the four-wheel-drives in large numbers. Their second thought was that parties of ramblers were about to tackle Pig Hill, but the lack of red socks, grim expressions and maps in plastic cases worn like magic amulets soon disabused them of that idea. Then when everybody came into church, and they ran out of hymn books and had to share, and prayer books and had to share them too, they were seriously disconcerted.

The singing was louder than anything that had been heard in the village since the milk lorry met a man with a dog and had to sound its horn; people were raising their hands in praise, and the regulars were wondering who they were waving to. Adrian, faced with a full church for the first time since New Year 2000, preached such a sermon that when he asked everybody to get up out of their seats, the cracking of arthritic joints was like machine-gun fire.

Everybody seemed to enjoy it except the treasurer, who saw the seam on the collection bag splitting and remarked gloomily that they might need a new one, and Mrs Baring, who remarked that getting rid of one evangelical seemed to have left the way open for any number of others to jump in and fill the void.

'It could be like this every week,' I said. 'If the service was a bit more modern . . .'

'But it wouldn't be Our Little Church,' she said.

I sighed.

Chapter 16

St Patrick's breakfast plate

How much sensation can one little village take? I heard stories of how I'd rounded up whole gangs of ruffians (single-handed by most accounts; Jason and Lennox seemed not to get much of a look-in), exposed a plot to blow up the church, and generally wore my pants outside my trousers like a proper superhero. And when I put the record straight (but not so straight I wasn't still a bit of a hero) everyone seemed to turn their anger on the squatters, and said what a nice village it was before they came, and how much nicer it would be if only someone would do something to make them go away. They didn't have long to wait.

The battle for Vineyard Cottage was on a Saturday, the day after the Brigadier's funeral. The *Blicester Bugle* always says: 'The funeral arrangements were satisfactorily carried out by A Dolt and Son', but this is hardly ever true. Henry Dolt, son of the late Albert, and the third generation of Dolts in the funeral business, is an amiable man in white-haired middle age, always slightly lugubrious, as if that was part of the job. Over the years, he has never ceased to surprise me with the original way he conducts funerals. If his bearers actually wore red noses, baggy trousers and shoes two feet long, at least we'd know what to expect. As it is, we're on tenterhooks, wondering what bizarre twist he will bring to the proceedings. In the past he has, at different times, engraved the wrong name on a brass plate, changing the gender of the deceased; left a mourning family behind so that they missed the funeral altogether; fallen into the grave (a good one, that – he looked like the captain of the *Titanic* going down with his ship); and on one memorable occasion he brought a casket of somebody else's ashes to the funeral instead of the coffin. The widow saw him open the back of the hearse and produce a small wooden box on a velvet cushion. She lifted her veil, peered at it, and said, 'I remember him as being taller than that.'

The Brigadier's funeral, being a military occasion, and in the crypt too, provided unprecedented possibilities for screwing up. I remarked to Hilary over breakfast that if anybody even looked as though they might fire a salute, I would run away and leave them to it. The boys asked whether, in the event of my getting shot, they could have my collection of aliens out of the Shreddies packets. But there were no guns, and I was grateful for it. Blicester British Legion did the Brigadier proud. They turned out in force, with banners on parade, their medals gleaming in the lamplight, to say goodbye to a respected comrade. 'I vow to thee, my country' was sung with real gusto, and in my address I spoke of the Brigadier's devotion to duty, his love of all things African, and his determination to kill them, right up to the end.

And then Henry's men, solemn in their grey suits and black overcoats, shouldered the coffin, and carried it up the aisle, and with a couple of shuffling right-angle turns, across the back, and down the side aisle to the Chapel of St Botulus, where the hole in the floor gaped blackly. The congregation did a smart turn to the right to observe the proceedings. I had no idea how Henry had planned to manage this with dignity and decorum, and rather feared that neither would be on the agenda. The coffin was placed on the floor, and two of the bearers disappeared down the hole into the Hollywoods' crypt. I said the prayer of committal. A British Legion bugler, his chest heaving with the emotion and effort, played the Last Post in a shower of stunned bats, falling from the rafters. The two bearers at the top lifted the end of the coffin, tipping it into the hole. There were muffled cries of 'To me! To me!' and 'Take the weight!' and 'Up your end!' from the crypt. The coffin, now in a vertical position, wobbled alarmingly. Then it disappeared, and there was a muffled crash, and some unseemly language. There is something about the Hollywoods' crypt that encourages unseemly language. I gave Dennis at the organ the internationally recognized hand signal for 'Play *Nimrod* fortissimo' and he obliged, drowning out the sounds of splintering that were emerging from the dark vault. Henry stared impassively ahead. I knew he would say afterwards, because he always does, 'I thought that went pretty well, all things considered.'

The two bearers emerged from the crypt,

festooned with cobwebs and covered in dust, their hair tousled and full of small lumps of stone and plaster. As they brushed each other down, and formed up with their colleagues to march out of church two by two, something caught my eye, pink and white, lying in a trouser turn-up. It was a set of false teeth.

The Battle of Vineyard Cottage lasted ten minutes, maximum. The arrest of two of the squatters had shortened the odds considerably. What was interesting was that they immediately asked to see their solicitor. And what was even more interesting, apart from the fact that a couple of bikers had a solicitor at all, was that he turned out to be David Mortimer, of Pules, Mortimer and Nutleg.

I was on my way to Pighill, that Saturday morning, but I had to wait while a big yellow truck delivered a skip onto the grass in front of Vineyard Cottage, carefully not squashing the Harleys. A head looked out from one of the upstairs windows. It must be hard to look dishevelled when your head is shaved bald, but he managed it. The driver unhooked the chains from the skip, retracted his hydraulics, gave me an apologetic wave, and drove off down the village. A skip is always a bit of an event, because it's seen in the village as the opportunity for everybody to dispose of all the junk even the Scouts won't have for their jumble sale, and they aren't fussy. A skip on a Saturday would be a real bonus.

Off I went on my way, and thought no more about it, until eleven o'clock, by which time I was home, underlining the parts of my sermon for the next day where the theology was a bit weak, so I'd need to shout.

The battle began just as the church clock struck eleven. The Major only had six people to help him, but had, of course, planned it with military precision. What I didn't see, watching from the bottom of the drive, I was told about afterwards. As soon as one of the female squatters appeared in the back garden, lured there on some pretext to get the back door open, the signal was given. Two black-clad figures, wearing crash helmets over woollen masks and armed with a pair of bolt-cutters, ran up to the front of the cottage, snipped the security chains from two of the bikes, and tinkered them into life. Then, revving loudly, and with an ancient ceremonial gesture of derision towards the house, they rode off calmly up the road, past the church and out of sight.

Within seconds, all six remaining squatters ran from the house shouting, squeezing past each other to get out of the front door, the two men pulling on helmets. They mounted the two remaining bikes, each with a girl on the pillion, and roared off in pursuit. Immediately, the front door closed behind them, and the other two girls were left outside. A top window opened, and from it came a shower of clothes, CDs, bottles and hairbrushes, handbags, and an air rifle, all landing in the skip on the grass below the window. The girls were helpless, torn between watching their belongings raining into the skip, and their friends disappearing off into the distance, and then they began turning the air blue. Some of their language, I have to say, was completely new to me, an ordinary country parson who doesn't watch very much Channel 4. Then one girl leapt into the skip to retrieve their handbags, and the other rushed up and banged on the door. But two more figures in black appeared from the side of the house, wielding large metal bars, and I began to worry that a real fight was about to start. Blessed are the peacemakers, I thought, so long as they don't get caught in the crossfire.

All four bikes returned, with a rider apiece. They had been abandoned only a few hundred yards up the road. A police van appeared. The metal bars were pushed through the spokes of the Harleys' rear wheels. Nobody was going anywhere, and the battle was over. Even when something does happen in Cheeving, it doesn't last very long.

Major Stern himself came round from the back

of his house, looking, well, stern, but pleased with himself, nevertheless.

'We'll have the police on you!' roared one of the squatters. 'We've got rights!'

More policemen than have ever been in the village in all its history were emerging from the van. The bikers seemed to deflate.

'Inspector!' called a voice from the cottage window. 'I think you should see this!' The voice was coming from behind a spiky-looking pot plant. The senior police officer was let in through the front door. The bikers checked to see if a quick getaway was possible, but the bikes were effectively immobilized.

The men were handcuffed. There would be charges of grievous bodily harm, criminal damage, growing pot plants, and owning white powders of varying degrees of illegality. The two bike thieves arrived back on foot, and the four figures who had secured the house from the back emerged from the front door.

One of the squatters turned on the Major.

'Mr Big, aren't you? You couldn't shift us without half a dozen men!'

'Which men would they be?' the Major asked calmly.

Crash helmets came off. Balaclava masks were removed. Long hair was shaken out. All six of the Major's troops were clearly of the female persuasion.

'This will look good when the word gets around,' said the Major, 'that you were evicted by women.'

'Good morning, Vicar,' he called, when the police van had gone, but I was still watching to see if anything else might happen. 'Thank you for going to see young Jamie. He really appreciated it.'

'Welcome home,' I said. 'That was neatly done. Who are your friends?'

'Police and army. Joint operation,' he said. 'Everybody thinks that just because I've been in Belize, I haven't a clue what's going on. Been liaising with the police, and they've been keeping an eye on that lot for months. Just needed to catch them with the stuff on them. And you did a good job last night, yourself.'

'It'll be quieter now they're gone,' I said.

'Don't count on it,' he said. 'I might be into military bands, but I still play them bloody loud.'

The arrest of Sir Samuel Saneway, reported in the papers after the weekend, caused yet another sensation, but only second hand. Reading about it and watching it happen are two different things. But there we were in the national press, our little village waving furiously, gurning and mouthing 'Hello, Mum.' After all that excitement, the village took some impressing, and seeing its name in print was just the thing. Only a complete ass would say that nothing ever happens in Cheeving Halfpenny. Shares in Saneways Supermarkets plummeted, and Jim Donovan bought lots. Sir Samuel was released on bail, Somerbury's put in a bid to buy out Saneways, the shares rocketed, and Jim sold them. We heard nothing more about a supermarket in our village. Nor a community centre, and definitely no new church. A few months later, the rumour went round that a field at Pighill had been bought by agents working for Somerbury's. I'll keep you posted.

Chapter 17

Lettuce with a gladsome mind

Baby Dilip's baptism was the high point of morning service, and the usual congregation was augmented by the Gruntles and their friends. There was hardly a seat to be had, and the choir was looking particularly pleased with itself, because it at least had elbow room. Fortunately, I'm not one of those vicars that make you sing 'Wide, wide as the ocean' with actions, or there would have been a nasty outbreak of black eyes.

Dilip was a stout tot by now, and as I hefted him over the font, in the special grip they teach you at Theological College, he reached up with one chubby hand, and grabbed my nose. The congregation, gathered around, smiled, but he didn't let go; in fact, he sunk his tiny fingernails in so hard I was obliged to try and prise them out with my free hand, which was a bit like trying to shake off an octopus. Smiles turned to chuckles as, tears running down my cheeks, I eventually lowered Dilip until he was practically swinging from my nose with one hand. At last he let go, still smiling. By this time the congregation was rolling about on the floor, helpless with mirth; all the people with videos were working out how much they could sell

the footage for to *You've Been Framed*, and my
nose was probably scarred for life.

I baptized him Dilip Edward Paul, gave his
godfather a candle lit from the big one left over
from Easter, and passed him back to Karen, or
Shanti, or both.

Before we left the church, Ted announced in
stentorian tones that everyone was invited to The
Stag after the service to celebrate Dilip's christening.
There was a general murmur of approval, once
people had remembered what The Stag was.

Dennis lined up the choirboys who had sung
flat, to be thrashed or spared as I saw fit, but I
was feeling in a mellow mood, and gave them all
the thumbs-up. Dennis grumbled that it would
do them no good in the long term, and put his
implements away.

Outside, while every possible combination of
baby, mother, godparents and Vicars was being
photographed, I remarked to Ted that there didn't
seem to be a full turnout of Gruntles.

'True,' he conceded, 'which is why I invited all
the congregation. A lot I'd invited aren't here. Some
rang and said they couldn't come, and some just
haven't turned up. Paul says he's going to be busy
on the farm, cludgering at the new field, but that's
a load of horse feathers, and he knows I know it.
Field will still be there tomorrow. Nobody's going
to nick it, are they? While my cousin Steve reckons
his new wife won't let him drive over this far in the
Sunday traffic. She's his third, and they've all been
odd 'uns. And my sister Edna says she won't leave

the new puppies. All a lot of tosh. You coming
down the pub with us? And your wife and boys?'

'Will there be enough?' I asked.

'With so many staying away, them as does come
can eat like princes!' he laughed.

I said we'd be there. And we were.

The baptism party had the room at the back,
and the front bar was full of the usual Sunday
lunchtime crowd. Ted had a word with Arthur, and
all the food was brought into the front bar, so that
everyone could get stuck in. For once, if anybody
was on a diet, nobody thought to remember it.
Shanti and Dilip were the centre of attention, with
Dilip showing an impressive capacity for sheer
hard sleep in what was becoming a noisier crowd
all the time. Alan and Mary were there, Alan still

limping slightly, but then he'd been told he might always limp. Jason and Melony, Derek Morris and his wife whose name I can never remember, Big Jim Donovan, John and Mrs Goddard and Myrtle, Mrs General, the whole church choir, the band of the Blues and Royals, the Sealed Knot, the Royal Horticultural Society, the staff of Harrods, the cast of *Emmerdale* and the crew of HMS *Hermes* all seemed to be there. Hilary tried once or twice to stop the boys making pigs of themselves, and then let them get on with it so she could enjoy herself.

There were almost as many people behind the bar as around it, with Arthur and his staff pulling pints until they had arms like Popeye, milking the optics, and wading in a growing heap of juice bottle tops.

Major Stern was drinking gin and telling a group of grateful villagers that Belize is a swamp on the outside, and a jungle on the inside, it's hot and it rains a lot, and there are mosquitoes that can suck you empty and *then* give you malaria, and on the whole, he'd rather be in Cheeving Halfpenny. And somebody asked whether he even noticed the difference, and it wasn't that funny, but we all laughed anyway.

A couple of passing cyclists in lycra tights were pulled from their bicycles and given pints of beer and chicken legs. People who had just gone down the road for a Sunday paper were hauled into The Stag, given drinks and plates and told to help themselves. Huge amounts of food seemed to be eaten, but the buffet didn't seem to be getting any smaller. Both bars were full, and Ted, so he said with a huge smile, was in heaven. I squeezed my way through the crush to Jason. Melony had a drink in one hand, a vol-au-vent in the other, and was balancing her plate on her bust, which is a pretty impressive feat.

'You were asking where heaven is,' I said. 'According to Ted, it's here, now.'

Jason looked at his drink, damaged a scotch egg, and said, 'I'd go along with that. Free beer and food, and everybody smiling. But what about hell?'

Just visible, outside the door of the pub, in the November cold, was Paul Gruntle. He was eating a packet of crisps he'd obviously paid for, and drinking what looked horribly like orange squash. I made my way out to him. He greeted me with a nod, his face expressionless.

'Not joining the party?' I asked him, although it was pretty obvious he wasn't.

'I've got a field to cludger this afternoon,' he said. 'This will do me.'

'On a Sunday? Think of the Sunday drivers!' The cludger is as wide as God's mercy and travels along the road at walking pace. That isn't my walking pace, mind, but the older Miss Tredgett's, Mollence, who always gets up first to go to the communion rail, and won't let anyone overtake her, so the whole process takes ten minutes longer than it should. I tried again.

'But it's Sunday, and a party, and your nephew's just been baptized.'

He snorted. 'All right for Dad, wasting his

money on people. Did I get a party for my twenty-first? "Things are a bit tight," he said then.'

'Don't be an arse,' I said. 'Come in, have a proper drink and join the party.'

He shook his head. 'She can make a fool out of Dad, but she won't make a fool out of me.'

I reported back to Jason. 'That's where hell is,' I said, nodding towards the back of Paul's head. 'The same place as heaven, but refusing to join the party.'

Doctor Kelly was in the middle of the throng, with a little space all around him. He usually drinks alone because he doesn't believe in dentists, and certainly wouldn't go to one even if he admitted they might exist, so he has teeth like liquorice allsorts and breath that can (and on one memorable occasion did) stop a clock.

'And what diet are you on, Vicar?' he asked cheerfully. I told him about the twenty-six-day diet, and how I was on B for the third time round, which meant I could have beer, or beef and beans and broccoli. But right now, I was having a beer.

'And is it working?' he asked. 'Is there any less of you in the trouser department?'

I had to admit there wasn't. He sighed deeply. Several flies fell dead from mid-air.

'I tell all my patients to lose a few pounds,' he said. 'Whatever they come in for, bunions, piles, sore throat, circumcision or phantom pregnancy. "Stop smoking, and lose a few pounds," I say.'

'So it's your fault the whole village is on a diet, is it?'

'No,' he said emphatically. 'You can't blame me for that. I tell people to lose a few pounds. And what do they do instead? They go on a diet. This diet, that diet, the hay diet, which only works if you're an actual horse, and that diet that lets you eat anything so long as it's fried. And do they lose weight? Not so that you'd notice.'

He took a sip of his whisky, and went on.

'Everybody insists that their diet is the best one, and some say their diet is the only one. But do you ever hear anybody say, "My, you look fit and well – whatever diet you're on, I want some of that"? No, you don't. Because it isn't dieting that makes the difference, it's losing weight. Forget the diet, Vicar. Just lose a few pounds.'

I was just thinking how good it would be to just go back to enjoying food without having to look it up in the dictionary, when the party caught up with me. Derek Morris eased his way through the crush to me, waving a chicken leg.

'Vicar!' he said. 'You did me a turn when you recommended young Jason to me.'

'You're keeping him on, then?'

'Oh, yes,' he said. 'I had a real cash-flow problem until Jason took things in hand. And he's a good mechanic, too.'

I told him that since I'd made Jason a sidesman, collections were up nearly twelve per cent, but I didn't mention that most of his talents in the mechanical department had been learned starting cars when the keys had been unavailable, on account of the owners having them in their pockets.

Hilary came elbowing her way through the crowd, an alarmed look on her face.

'Have you seen the time?' she asked.

There was no point in looking at the pub clock. Just as the pub still serves beer in pints, so the clock only gave the time in old Imperial units, and was not to be relied on. My watch said it was ten to six. As it was dark outside, I believed it. The whole afternoon had gone by and nobody had even noticed.

'Evensong!' she reminded me. I looked around. The only person I couldn't see was Dennis, the organist, who must have crept off, a slave to duty, and would now be playing that mood music organists do to cover up the sound of people complaining that the church heating isn't up to scratch. I collared a passing chorister, and sent him up the road.

'Find Dennis,' I said to him. 'Tell him to turn off the lights, lock up the organ, and get down here and play the piano. We can have the service here.'

Off the little fellow scampered, and back he came before you could say Psalm 119, with Dennis, his black gown billowing around him like Batman's cape. We sat him at the piano, and he cracked his knuckles, tried a few arpeggios, decided they were stale and he'd rather have a bag of crisps, and then bashed out the tunes of well-known hymns. And we all joined in, and God was praised, and that's about it, really.

An Invitation to JOIN THE FRIENDS OF

SCM-CANTERBURY PRESS

And save money on your religious book buying ...

Friends of SCM-Canterbury Press is a superb value-for-money membership scheme offering massive savings on both imprints.

BENEFITS OF MEMBERSHIP

- *Exclusive: 20% off all new books published in the year*
- *Exclusive: offers at 50% or more off selected titles from the backlist*
- *Exclusive: offers on Epworth Press and other distributed lists*
- *Exclusive: dedicated website pages, e-mail bulletins, special offers and competitions*

Join now – and start saving money on your book-buying today!

If you would like to join please contact:
The Mailing List Secretary, SCM-Canterbury Press,
9-17 St Albans Place, London N1 ONX
Tel: 00 44(0) 207 359 8034 • Fax: 00 44 (0) 207 359 0049
Email: office@scm-canterburypress.co.uk
PLEASE QUOTE BOOKAD

Alternatively why not join online and gain an extra saving of £2; the members' pages are very easy to use and all online ordering is completely secure.

Join at: www.scm-canterburypress.co.uk
Subscriptions run annually.

2005 Rates: UK £8.00 • International: £10.00